Selected Plays

Photo by Carl Gibson

Cathy Crabb is a playwright, poet, screenwriter, journalist and lyricist who has written more than thirty plays for the stage. She lives in Oldham with her husband Carl.

By the author from Flapjack Press

Beside the See-Side
MUMB
Selected Plays

CATHY CRABB
SELECTED PLAYS

Flapjack Press
flapjackpress.co.uk
Exploring the synergy between performance and the page

Published in 2024 by Flapjack Press
Salford, Gtr Manchester
⊕ flapjackpress.co.uk · **f** Flapjack Press
𝕏 FlapjackPress · ▶ flapjackpress2520

ISBN 978-1-8384703-7-1

Cover photo by Camille Roux on Unsplash
⊕ unsplash.com/@camilleroux_com

Design and illustrations by Paul Neads
⊕ paulneads.co.uk

Printed by Imprint Digital
Exeter, Devon
⊕ digital.imprint.co.uk

This collection is dedicated to those people lucky enough to know the beauty and complexity of the neurodivergent mind.

Contents

Nota bene

Foreword

Some people outside of Manchester might name the likes of Simon Stephens or Jim Cartwright as the most iconic playwrights of our region, but if you ask any artist from Manchester who their favourite playwright is they may well say Cathy Crabb.

Cathy is a local legend, a truly unique playwright and poet, who's been a favourite of North West audiences for years. She has an incredible ability to write characters who are complex, nuanced, funny and remind you of real people you know. Even her more villainous characters like The Bubbler still retain their humanity, and you are surprised to end up understanding why they might have ended up as bitter and twisted as they are. Her dialogue is poetic and hilarious in equal measure and her work always makes me cry with laughter, before it invariably makes me sob with emotion too. If there was one thing that unites all of Cathy's work, from *Five Women: Rambling*, to *Beautiful House*, to *Twirlies and Girlies*, is that it is full of heart. Much like Cathy herself, who is the most generous artist, always has time to support others, and has been nurturing new playwrights around the region for years. I have been lucky enough to work with her and be inspired by her many times myself.

Let's hope this collection reaches more directors and theatres around the region and they restage some of these classics. I know I would love to watch every single one of them so I can laugh and cry at them all over again.

Lindsay Williams
Producer & Writer

Introduction

Yes, there's an Introduction. Don't feel you have to read it though. In fact, this is probably only really of interest to working class mums (born or trans women) who are neurodivergent and write plays.

Currently, you can count successful, known, neurodivergent, working-class, female playwrights with three children, who live in council property with a partner on low income who has supported them all their lives on one finger. But don't worry though, I'm out here seeking you out, championing you, and helping you as much as people have helped me.

But in case I haven't found you yet, here are some tips.

At first, I used to work when my kids were in bed and in that way I had a good sleep routine for them. I taught myself to touch type so that in the day, if I was writing, I could tell them off at the same time.

Wherever you go, whatever you do, look for narrative. I was inspired to write *Beautiful House* from taking my kids to Manchester Museum. It was also inspired by being unable to afford a mortgage, whilst buying the weekend *Guardian* (with their expensive property articles in early 2000s). I wrote the *Breastfeeding* sketch after being unable to breastfeed and a doctor accusing me of child abuse for not doing it. I wrote *The Bubbler* from my experience of living in pubs. And other plays are inspired by things you don't need to know. I don't need to know your dark or beautiful (or both) inspirations either.

Start reviewing. You won't get paid, but you can always have a free night/day out at least once a month. And you'll go and see things that you wouldn't normally be interested in. Once, at Halloween, Carl and I went to watch a soprano wailing over a black and white film of an abandoned house. It was good, in a way.

Don't waste time reading a million books on how to write. You probably see the world much differently than those people. You probably write in a way they wouldn't really get. Learn in the same way you decided what you want your bedroom to look like, like when you fixed *that thing*, like when you made *that* tea for the first time and everyone loved it. It's only through doing what you think you can do that you learn how to do it. There's loads of plays in here; practise by taking one of the short ones and changing the subject or the theme. Like, instead of Melody Coffey the breastfeeding expert, it's Joanna Royce the health and safety officer. Or Mike Larry the speeding course leader. Actually go through it and redo every line with this in mind. And – *shazam!* – you've written a little play. Put your own work on at first and bring your own crowd. That's the best way to start. Then you'll see if people like it or not. Find a pub, club, spare room and do it that way. The permission is never going to come.

Find your way to get it from your head to the stage. Invite me please. I'll always come and watch if I can. And don't you dare ever stop writing when you love it so much.

Finally, a note to anyone wanting to perform any of these plays – fill your boots. But make sure you pay me. I got bills.

Cathy Crabb
June 2023

Premiered at Studio Salford, 2004

"The inspiration for this piece was my MA in Contemporary Theatre, where I studied the style and plays of Beckett. I realised, when studying, we were kind of clutching at straws to define writers sometimes, and we'd go deep into their likes and dislikes, like obsessive superfans. It's also inspired by an enigmatic primary school headteacher in Royton, who had a unique way of talking when addressing children. She was the headteacher of the school my son Bobby went to. She was like Glenda the Good Witch – adorable, but you don't wanna mess with her. My mum and dad's pub raised a lot of money for the nursery of the school and she was really grateful. A lovely woman." *CC*

CAST (2)

MISS CRABB
A headteacher with a unique, low, deliberate, and excited high-pitched voice. You can tell she loves children, but you can also tell that this voice has been edited and perfected over the years.

MISS NELSON
A teacher who speaks with her eyes – let any child dare to whisper, sniff or breath! Her eyes sometimes ever so slightly say she doesn't quite agree with Miss Crabb, but they also say when she does.

SCENE 1

MISS CRABB: Could you turn the music off now Miss Nelson? Thank you. GOOD AFTERNOON EVERYBODY.

MISS NELSON: Good afternoon Miss Crabb, good afternoon everyone.

(Miss Crabb now addresses the audience as if it was a school assembly.)

MISS CRABB: Now last FRIDAY in our ASSEMBLY we were listening to GAELIC music. And Miss Fletcher's class were very excited because they had been watching RIVERDANCE that morning in the HALL. And if I remember rightly, AMIE MORRIS gave us an IMPROMPTU PERFORMANCE of IRISH DANCING, which I'm sure Michael Flatley would have been very impressed by, wouldn't he Miss Nelson?

(Miss Nelson smiles and nods.)

Now this week, in our assembly, we are listening to SCHUBERT. SCHUBERT was a COMPOSER. A COMPOSER is a MAN who can imagine lots and lots of musical notes, from lots and lots of musical instruments and he writes them down and he CREATES a BEAUTIFUL PIECE OF MUSIC.

The REASON why we are listening to SCHUBERT today is because SCHUBERT is the most favourite COMPOSER of the MAN who wrote the STORY which we will be LISTENING TO today. And that MAN is CALLED SAMUEL BECKETT. And the STORY is CALLED WATT.

Now – SAMUEL BECKETT was a WRITER. He was IRISH but he wanted to live in FRANCE. And that is where he LIVED until he DIED. And he is MOST FAMOUS for writing PLAYS.

SAMUEL BECKETT loved WORDS and he wrote lots and lots because SAMUEL BECKETT loved to WRITE WORDS DOWN.

SAMUEL BECKETT'S plays are VERY SPECIAL, because unlike Miss Nelson's NATIVITIES that make us feel GOOD about OURSELVES and GOD, SAMUEL BECKETT'S PLAYS make us feel GOOD about NOT BEING HIM. Or make us feel GOOD about NOT being the PEOPLE in the PLAY. They make us feel good by first feeling a little bit BAD.

Now this sounds a little bit SILLY and a bit HARD for us to UNDERSTAND. SO we are going to DO a little EXPERIMENT. I WANT YOU to WATCH Miss Nelson and do WHAT SHE DOES.

Miss Nelson, could you pick up the CHIPSTICKS that are in the BOWL on the FLOOR next to you, and everyone else do the same. Now – I want you to EAT the CHIPSTICKS.

(Pause while audience eats chipsticks from bowls next to their seats.)

How do we feel after THAT. I THINK that you FEEL very, very THIRSTY. Now – Miss Nelson, I want to pick up the CUP of WATER from the FLOOR next to you, and everyone else do the same. Now – I want you to DRINK the WATER.

(Pause while audience drinks the water.)

How do we feel NOW. I THINK that you FEEL much, much BETTER.

Now – SAMUEL BECKETT'S plays make you FEEL like the little bit of time AFTER the CHIPSTICKS and BEFORE the drink of WATER.

And this may be a little bit hard for you to UNDERSTAND right NOW but ONE DAY you might GO and SEE a SAMUEL BECKETT PLAY and you will COME OUT and you will THINK to YOURSELF 'OH YES! MISS CRABB WAS RIGHT! THAT IS EXACTLY HOW I FEEL!'

Now before we listen to the story of WATT please remember that NEXT FRIDAY we will all need to bring in a handbag because Miss Nelson is going to explain how our MUMMY's wombs or our carer's wombs – but not our DADDY'S or our male carer's wombs because they don't have one – are like a handbag and that is why LADIES like HANDBAGS. And she is going to do this so we can UNDERSTAND a little bit about the story of THE WHOLE WOMAN by a lady writer called GERMAIN GREER. NOW it might be one of YOUR MUMMY'S handbags or a SPORTS BAG, any kind of bag you can get apart from a plastic one because plastic bags are dangerous and we shouldn't play with them should we? But please remember your bags or you won't really be able to understand the story.

NOW let us LISTEN to the STORY of WATT. Miss Nelson, can you hold up the pictures please...

(Reads extract from Watt.)

(Lights fade after a considerable amount of reading time – enough to make the audience uncomfortable and bored.)

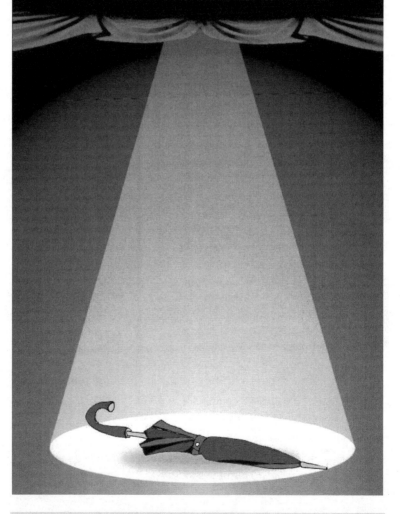

THE BUBBLER

"Crabb has succeeded in putting across points about politics, young people and the arts in an entertaining way."
David Chadderton, British Theatre Guide

Premiered at Studio Salford, 2012

The Bubbler is set in a time and place where art is seen as frivolous, where greed is encouraged, and where bar staff bear the brunt.

"Happiness and unhappiness collide throughout this play, and that should be the overriding atmosphere." *CC*

> "The rain it raineth on the just
> And also on the unjust fella;
> But chiefly on the just, because
> The unjust hath the just's umbrella."
> —*Lord Bowen (1835-1894)*

CAST (2)

PETER

Aged in his 40s, Peter has the air of a man who has a wealth of empathy for himself alone. No one has had a worse course of life than him and he has to get up every day with the knowledge that he works in his job for his sins: he loved his old boss but couldn't turn down the flattery of sleeping with his workforce and so lost his much-loved position at the bank. In those days the world was his oyster and he made the most of everything, with a wife tending to him and his friends' adoration. Things have since slipped away or been shattered. His descent into working for Cash Generator resembles the fall of Satan, and is very much like Milton's Satan ["Better to reign in Hell than serve in Heaven." John Milton, *Paradise Lost* (1.263)]. His past life has left him aware that he is paying the price for something, and he feels that people truly sell their souls to him when they turn up with stolen goods. He sometimes mulls over, chews, and then spits out things that are said to him in his own way, which is usually with contempt. He thinks he hides his jealously or admiration for others well, but is betrayed by his choice of words.

PAUL

A man in his 30s, to whom the world is an amazing place, holding promise and fascination. When he was at school, he didn't want anyone to know he was interested in poems or stories, although he wrote both and loved learning about them. He now sees that as something to repair, and also to repair damage he may have caused to others by making fun of them if they did anything artistic. He has made his peace with those people and is thought of very fondly by most – apart from the odd girl he has spurned. He is a self-taught musician, knows many other musicians, and loves music of all kinds. He can play the trumpet extremely well, as well as a bit of guitar, plays in a band, and also frequently as a session musician. Paul tries to see the good in everyone, as that makes him feel good. But this is invariably tested with Peter. He does share Peter's empathy for himself and he is not his most annoying customer by a long shot. In fact, trying to turn Peter's moods and moans around is an unhealthy challenge for him, although he hasn't yet succeeded. He also allows himself the pleasure of encouraging Peter's anger and exasperation (a throw-back for him to his time making fun of arty types), and he supposes he laughs knowing he has moved on.

TONY RABBONI

An absent character (and an ancient name for Christ).

SCENE 1: PETER PAYS PAUL

Late afternoon in a bar in Manchester city centre. Not fashionable or expensive, a place for 'regulars'.

Music is playing on a CD player which occasionally sticks. There might be certain songs where it sticks on particular words, over and over, at appropriate places in the script.

Hooked onto the bar is a forgotten umbrella.

If possible, as the audience come in, the actor playing Paul will serve them drinks. After Paul has served the drinks, he reads the paper. He is reading something that is taking his face on a journey, really enjoying it, fascinated and laughing to himself. The door goes, or a familiar shuffle is heard. He looks up expectantly to see that it is Peter. His heart sinks.

In sidles Peter as if he may just piss all over everyone – he is that superior and that annoyed. Breathing is obvious from him but not fast – all his noises, grunts and sniffs are of someone who has been walking fast with earphones in. He might be wiping his nose, it may have been raining, but to the audience and to the world of the pub, you will flinch in case snot or a slap swings your way. He gets to the bar and takes the whole thing up, as if he is gripping it like a buoy.

Paul has his eye on the drink stirrers – he usually moves them before Peter comes in and he's forgotten, because Peter has a habit of banging one on the bar like he is playing a drum.

>   **PETER:** Fucking scrotes.

>   **PAUL:** Bitter Peter?

>   **PETER:** No, I'm chirpy and loving life... I don't want bitter anyway, I want something else

(Paul readies himself to make a suggestion.)

>   Oh I'll just have bitter... what's the guest ales?

(Paul goes to answer.)

>   I can't be arsed... bitter-bitter yeah. Don't mither me – bitter, hurry up.

(Paul laughs to himself about this incredulously – mainly due to the pointless flick-flacking.)

(Peter slaps a bag of pound coins onto the table, opens it, fiddles for the money and shifts it down the bar.)

(Paul hopes to sidle to the other end and resume his paper.)

(Peter is now mulling over something that is irking him and shaking his head until he gives in to it.)

You know, in my primary school, there was a lad who had pants made out of curtains.

PAUL: What were his curtains made out of?

(Peter stares at Paul, then drinks for a moment trying to calm down, still staring as Paul reads the paper uncomfortably.)

PETER: His curtains. Were non-existent. Because they were. His pants. And that is called 'poor'. No one is that poor now.

PAUL: Well, that's something then I suppose?

PETER: But they want you to think they are. I'll believe you're poor when I see you eating with the pigeons, or wearing your curtains. That's what should happen, not the spends they have. Not a bag of shopping for nothing.

PAUL: Had some tough customers today then?

(During Peter's following guttural tirade, Paul becomes utterly uncomfortable and upset inside, which bleeds out into his eyes in spite of himself.)

PETER: Lazy, scrawny, druggie bastards. Fucking-horrible-scumbag-looting-Gregg-pasty-pinching-Maccy-D-munching-knuckle-dragging-state-scrounging-stinking-oxygen-wasters.

(Thinks for a moment.)

Utter waste of life, time, space. Weedy skunk-wreaking-knob-sucking vermin. A dirty protest by God. A skid mark on the city. A piss stain on the public. Should have been thrown onto the fire as foetus.

(Pause.)

Course in your job you don't have to deal with dickheads, do you?

PAUL: No, no I don't, I'm lucky me.

PETER: Well, maybe drunks but – that's different. I tell you, they were lucky when they got me in there. Never mind the job centre advert asking for 'Someone who goes the extra mile, with a passion for working in a fun, vibrant environment'. It is merely the selling on of poisoned shite from moronic loooosers. If it weren't for me, there could have been some nasty unsympathetic bastard doing my job. It's a wonder these eyes have any shine left.

PAUL: Yeah. Must be hard, keeping a sparkle to them. What's hot at the minute then?

PETER: There's a big wave of gardening equipment, I can't even tell you, it's a huge clunking big fuck off wave of lawn mowers, strimmers, hammers, trowels. It travels out of the sheds of the forgetful and insecure and joins up together in a ginnel and slunks off straight into the back of a scrote's van, off to us – bought again, back in an unsafe shed, off again, it's a metal mud-soaked caterpillar in and out in and out.

PAUL: Wouldn't have thought you had that much gardening stuff come in.

PETER: There you go.

PAUL: Thought it was mainly phones and X-boxes.

PETER: There you go you, see. It's varied and challenging. We have one who comes in every other week with a load of shit like that, all slit scars like up his arms. Arms like a lattice pie. He brings all sorts – scythes, big spades and forks. The 'self-farmer' we call him. Just let me leave it behind anyway, they've drove me mad today.

(Half-pause.)

Some scumbag comes in trying to sell some stepladders, coppers come in behind him, he pretended he was an electrician and got up them to change the light bulb. I had to go along with it because I rely on him this time of the week – he's one of me regulars. And I don't like to be dishonest you know, I don't like to collude. Never go collude with your customers. I like to be fair and just. Is this your umbrella?

PAUL: No, I left it there in case the guy came back in for it.

PETER: Oh right.

PAUL: It's Tony's, do you know him?

PETER: What's his second name?

PAUL: Rabonni.

PETER: Tony Rabonni, cracking. His name rings a bell. Does he come in a lot then?

PAUL: No two nights a week, sometimes just one.

PETER: Work in town, does he?

PAUL: Yeah, well, he works all over the place, I think.

PETER: I wreak of them today. One comes in with a bundle of cards he's had since he was a kid – unbelievable – Pokemon. I said 'Sorry son, I can't buy them off you, but you might be able to get swapsies at Forbidden Planet.' Then some mithering slag comes in – 'That's my ring in the window' – jibbering, trying to stand up to me, shaking, she goes 'That ring there, you've bought that from my son – he's fifteen you know.' I said 'Oh is he now? So he's selling stolen property is he?' She scuttled off and I took it out the window, I'll sell it myself. I only gave him £20 and it's worth about £300. If I sell it for £150, that's good for me that. The little weasel that sold it me... anyway I want to forget now.

(Something sticks here, or an inappropriate song comes on, or something else which is a good few seconds' distraction for both.)

What does he do, umbrella man?

PAUL: Well, he's er... he works at a mental health charity...

PETER: Right.

PAUL: ...And he's a musician.

PETER: Eh?

PAUL: He does both.

PETER: Why would he do both? One must be his job and the other his hobby.

PAUL: Well, I talk to him a lot and he seems quite serious about both.

PETER: No, no, let's have it right. He's a molly-coddler of the comatosed. And he likes to play the... what?

PAUL: He plays a few things.

PETER: Right.

PAUL: Yeah, he plays – so he tells me anyway – he plays the harmonica, the drums –

PETER: Okay, so he's a volunteer hugger and he does a one-man band does he?

PAUL: No, he – not together, or maybe together an' all but, he plays... he has a band and he's a session musician. Guitar, drums, clarinet, trumpet –

PETER: You know a lot about the many instruments he plays, don't you?!

PAUL: He's an interesting bloke. He's played here a few times... Not a bad way to earn your money is it?

PETER: Good job if you can get it...

(Starts singing 'Money for Nothing' by Dire Straits.)

'That ain't workin', that's the way you do it. Play the guitar on the MTV…'

(Then sings, very high-pitched like Sting, and straight into Paul's face.)

'I WANT MY – I WANT MY – I WANT MY MTV.' I wonder what he's best at, the guitar or wiping people's arses? My bet is the arses.

(Paul's worst-case scenario now happens as Peter picks up a drink stirrer and begins tapping it on the bar – he then gets two of them to show he could have a go at the drums if he chose to.)

PAUL: He's a nice fella actually –

PETER: Well – I mean – guitars and gimps.

PAUL: I think he does alright you know?

PETER: Yeah right.

PAUL: He just does a bit of everything, and keeps busy.

PETER: Hmmm.

(Pause.)

So… is he married this bloke?

PAUL: No…

PETER: Hmmmm.

PAUL: He has a partner but don't think they are married.

PETER: Right. Support him in his tinkering with this and that does she?

PAUL: Think so…

PETER: Scrounging off a woman? Very gallant.

PAUL: Oh support him? Nah, he supports her I think, she's an artist, she's just getting her career off the ground and that.

PETER: Off the ground… off the ground… you have to get to a stage in life where you decide that you've done enough messing about and just fucking knuckle down and get on with it. I can't be doing with all that me. We need to keep everything ticking over, there's no room now for mulling – trying things out. You work, very hard, all the time. And that's that… kids these days… fucking playing at life they are. It's one big daydream through the window to them.

PAUL: He int a kid, he's a bit younger than you and a bit older than me. Anyway, it's good if you can do what you enjoy, it's not doing any harm is it?

PETER: Pays well does it? Bar work?

PAUL: Well, while people are drinking, I'm in work...

PETER: But you can't get many tips and that.

PAUL: Not really, no.

PETER: You don't get any from me.

PAUL: No.

PETER: And if I'm a good reflection –

PAUL: Yeah –

PETER: You mustn't do that well.

PAUL: Sometimes, but you can't rely on them.

PETER: Nah. Still, why should you?

PAUL: Yeah, exactly.

PETER: I don't.

PAUL: No.

PETER: I mean I do get some treats me, bubble some of them now and again. That's between you, me, and the authorities that. I just help them out, you know. One hand washes the other. Works well for me that. I shop 'em in, they ignore my dealings. Just wish I could have... the work's not coming in like it used to... I'm getting tired of it anyway, I'm tired and agitated by this never-ending torture, can't concentrate, I can't see meself properly... where've I gone... come on now Peter – come on.

SCENE 2: THE BATTLE BETWEEN RIGHT AND WRONG

PETER: You can't get tips off the mentally ill can you? That's for sure. Unless it's tips on how to argue with yourself.

PAUL: I think you get expenses sometimes.

PETER: Bet we have the same clientele –

PAUL: Sometimes he has to go to their homes –

PETER: Him and me. Boney Tony.

PAUL: He int boney.

PETER: Are you in love with him? You've not stopped talking about him since I came in... Why, what does he look like?

PAUL: Why?

PETER: You may as well go the whole hog now – describe him.

Short, tall?

PAUL: He's about average height.

PETER: One nil.

PAUL: He works out.

(Pause.)

There's a painting of him in the Bridgewater. His girlfriend did it, she's done it in like oils. It was in the paper. Anyway, the Bridgwater bought it from them and they gave the money to Centrepoint.

PETER: Wanker.

(Pause.)

PAUL: It's up to people what they do with their money.

PETER: I think me and him would have very different takes on things. If he saw the side I did, he'd do fuck all for them. One of my regulars – he's like your size, bit smaller – bitter please – he's always pulling his top down going like this – *(Does it.)* Like he's hiding himself.

PAUL: Sounds sad.

PETER: Yeah, proper saddo. His eyes are always watering.

PAUL: Crying?

PETER: I don't know, wouldn't put it past him. But this is the face I do when I'm talking to him –

(Shows him.)

This is the face I have, and I talk like this – 'Hiya pal, you okay? Come and have a chat with Peter' see… I don't say 'Uncle Peter' because that's a bit – creepy – they're only kids. And I don't mind using me name, it means nothing to me that. And I give him five minutes to talk his crap before we get around to what he's brought this time.

PAUL: That's kind of you.

PETER: It's my remit. Empathy and concern goes a long way.

PAUL: Like a priest?

PETER: More like a pimp. I'm good with words. Remember what I said before? About the lawnmower caterpillar? You never heard anything like that before, have you?

PAUL: No. I'm just getting some lemons.

(Exits.)

(A song comes on that Peter sings along to, mumbling at first before he gets really into it, eventually getting up and dancing.)

(Paul enters with the lemons.)

So... what were you saying? About the crying lad?

PETER: Let's not call him the crying lad right? Let's call him the snivelling scrote, yeah?

PAUL: Well, I don't really want to call anyone that, sorry.

PETER: Listen, I'm just as bothered by these poor sods as anyone else, don't get me wrong. I can't bear to see what's happening to these kids. We should all do something, make a radical stand.

PAUL: Yes, we should help them in some way.

PETER: Or maybe instead of giving them a kiss, and a bag of shopping, we could slaughter them. Have a big cull, burn them and get rid of them like they did with the cows.

PAUL: Oh okay... you might be out of a job then.

PETER: And then you'd be out of a job an all. Fucking Tonio will still have a job though, won't he? Being as he's working for love and entertainment. Who's ever not wanting them two?

(Pause.)

(Peter looks very down; Paul cheers himself up by encouraging this malaise.)

PAUL: So, go on anyway, the lad who pulls his top down...

PETER: Yeah – he told me something. I took him to the chairs and gave it all the sympathetic father figure shite... I patted him on the shoulder, that's all, and this gave him some kind of green light to, as they say, open up. He said 'That is the first time someone has touched me for months.' He said 'I need a lot of attention, because I have never got over the loss' – get this, he goes – 'I have never got over losing my blanket' – I'm thinking, he can't be living rough – he goes 'When I was five, I left my blanket on the bus, and I've missed it ever since, but when I have a weed – that knot inside me of wanting my blanket goes away.'

PAUL: His blanket, like his covesy?

PETER: His what?

PAUL: His covesy.

PETER: What's one of them?

PAUL: That woolly thing you have from being a baby that you suck your thumb with.

PETER: It's not called that.

PAUL: Mine was.

PETER: Blankeys they're called.

PAUL: Yours was.

PETER: Everyone's was – blue with ribbon round the top that you sniffed.

PAUL: Oh right. Mine was white.

(Sucks on his pint and hugs the bar as if it is his blankey.)

PETER: But anyway, fucked up that innit? Carrying on about that in adulthood – what kind of sad excuse is that?

PAUL: Probably more to it than that, maybe that's when his Mum and Dad split up or something.

PETER: Well, let's leave the delving, shall we? If I felt sorry for them, I wouldn't be able to make a living out of them, would I?

PAUL: Well – you would, but it's hard. There's people come in here I feel sorry for and –

PETER: How d'you get round it then, I'm interested?

PAUL: Well, you just have to think that you are doing them a favour – even though they are annoying, and you don't share their views, you... just serve them and do your best to see a good side to them.

PETER: Sometimes that's impossible.

PAUL: Sometimes, it is very challenging yes. But the charm of a person can often be the saving grace. And sometimes you can have fun picking on them a bit, if you know how to.

PETER: I'm with you there, make them sweat, make them wait, yeah, wind them up. Eh, don't be doing that with me!

PAUL: Wouldn't dream of it... I wonder if Tony is going to come back in later? He's up at the shelter tonight doing a song writing workshop...

PETER: How lovely.

PAUL: Yeah, and when it's done they're making a podcast for BBC Manchester.

PETER: All those talented musicians in the world trying to get on and he's having the walking dead on the radio?!

PAUL: Yeah, terrible really.

PETER: Good for me though, I'll have a load of triangles and bongos to flog in the morning, you wait and see.

PAUL: It's all good then.

SCENE 3: PETER'S MILTONIC FALL FROM GRACE

PAUL: I'm not in work tomorrow got the day off.

PETER: Oh aye. Wish I could have a day off.

PAUL: Yeah. Should be good. I'm going to –

PETER: If I miss one shift I'm down. One shift. Don't know what I'd do if I was ill me. Or a family member died. Anyway, mostly there's no call for it, soft arses looking for an excuse not to come in, get it all the time. 'I've got flu – cough cough.' You never see a monkey with a cold, do you?

PAUL: No. Funny you should say that because Tony like – we were on about yeah? – he was saying to me that he thinks monkeys are further up than us in evolution –

PETER: They're not.

PAUL: Well, they've got fur, we haven't –

PETER: Hmmm... it's not fur is it, they're just hairy.

PAUL: Like you say, they never seem to be ill.

PETER: If they were higher up than us they wouldn't let us dress them up and have them smoking, would they?

PAUL: Hmmm... that's not really their choice –

PETER: Oh for Christ... I wish I had your job and all I had to do was talk about the monkeys. Look, I want a quiet drink, keep meself to meself, I don't want to be bothered by monkeys.

(Paul is subtly amused and trying not to make anything of it.)

If you did my job, you wouldn't either...

(Mulls over the absolute quandary of life, death, good, bad – briefly and with no real thought.)

I know you think this bloke is interesting, but in ten years' time believe me he'll be... fed up and... shattered. Leave it Peter, just leave it. Their illnesses and their battery burn of self-pity and suffering is sticking to you a bit, that's all, but that is nothing to what you have to face in loss, nothing. Their dark flame is comforting; if you have to live in this pit then at least you have that.

PAUL: No, animals never seem to get colds... probably because they don't have a lot of physical contact – hugging or kissing or anything.

PETER: Ahh, now see, shush a minute now, see... that's where he might have a point there, in that way – they are further up than us. Every person that's mithered my state of mind in that way has wound up being party to my downfall. If we all just had it off in season, life would be a lot simpler.

PAUL: Not that easy to orchestrate.

PETER: Everything on display all given a proper time and had a go. No meals, no chatting. No sacking. In and gone.

PAUL: No sacking? That doesn't sound good.

(Pause.)

PETER: Let's just say, I had it made and then just because of my irresistible charm – I was robbed of a great job. I was soaring, up there. Climbing, me. He loved me, my boss. Told me I'd be off the counter soon enough. I was his favourite; he was readying me for the assistant manager's job. You would think though, wouldn't you, that your boss would be impressed by your prowess, how you could get the girls? What kind of a man thinks that sleeping with all of his workforce is a bad thing?

PAUL: A jealous man?

PETER: Yes! A very jealous man. He got his son in, I was next assistant manager and he swooped in, so I got all the girls onside to bring him down, the only way they can and no, his son wouldn't touch them – he shot off crying to his daddy and I got the sack. But I'm glad, most of the girls work for me now, better perks on this side of the fence. I still hate him though, because we got on so well and that. He's a very devious man. Very manipulative. He wore you down with his good nature, you ever known one of them? Too nice? Anyway, better to be the boss of CEXr than to serve on the counter at NatWest... So, what you doing tomorrow then?

PAUL: Me?

PETER: Yes, you said you were... what was it?

PAUL: I'm taking my girlfriend to Chetham's Library. She only moved here from Leeds a few months ago and she's never been and she wanted to see where Marx and Engels sat –

PETER: Don't bother, it's shit.

PAUL: Well, she's interested to see what it looks like inside.

PETER: It looks like an old pub with books in it you aren't allowed to read.

PAUL: I like it.

PETER: Take her to the World Buffet instead. But don't get her a drink from there, it's a fucking rip off. Go to the Shambles first, the wine's cheap and she'll think she's been somewhere oldy-worldy. There you go, sorted.

PAUL: Right.

PETER: You're welcome.

SCENE 4: IT POURS DOWN

The music reflects a slight revelation, maybe at the point when Peter realises he can bubble Tony and his partner.

Paul is busy putting knives and forks into serviettes for something to do.

PETER: You could go to the gallery.

PAUL: Yeah.

PETER: But I wouldn't recommend it.

PAUL: Right.

PETER: There's nothing in there that you couldn't see in TK Maxx. It's full of annoying shufflers with nothing better to do than pack a Tupperware box with egg and stare at someone else's hard work, daydreaming that they could do a better job.

PAUL: Don't you think it's good we have those works in Manchester?

PETER: You what? A giant nail brush and a cartoon of cats outside a pub? Fuck off! That downstairs bit, a car boot sale in glass cabinets. I didn't bother taking the kids further than the café, that was bad enough – four quid a brownie... what kind of level of bullshit do you need to learn to a tee so that you can make a giant nail brush that you aren't even allowed to touch? They must be laughing all the way to the bank. If I learnt that spiel I'd have all sorts. I need to get on that. I mean, I could do some social commentary me, if I learnt that language.

PAUL: You could do your lawnmower caterpillar for a start.

PETER: Hang on... Yeah, maybe you make the thing and work backwards to saying what it means. And then wheel it round to the gallery and go – how much for that? I could…

(Thinks and taps a stirrer on the bar.)

I could have a giant Pot Noodle on a wire going directly into the arm of a scarecrow… and what would that mean?

PAUL: Well, it could mean that music is…

PETER: No, I'm thinking like the scarecrow is one of the scumbags… yeah… or like I could have a load of pound coins at the bottom of a toilet.

PAUL: Filthy lucre.

PETER: Covered in pretend crap.

(Pause.)

(Peter rips a beer mat in half, gets out a pen, and draws on the exposed side – he could possibly write a message or cry for help on it, as well as the drawing, and drop it on one of the tables when he leaves.)

PAUL: You should have gone upstairs, there's a painting of Christ, it's amazing – all the symbols are there of his past and future. Mary's on the floor looking into a treasure chest with the myrrh in it and all that. She sees his shadow reflected on the wall. He's stood like this…

(Mimics Jesus in the painting.)

…his eyes are towards heaven, hands up in the air, no top on, cloth around his waist, hands outstretched, it's in Joseph's workshop, shavings all over the floor and on the wall four nails behind him.

PETER: Lazy bastard. Swanning around feeling sorry for himself. In the way. I hope, really hope, that Joseph made that table where they had the last supper…

PAUL: The last supper – da Vinci's…

PETER: Yeah, I really hope that was his table, he got no recognition that man –

PAUL: I'm not sure da Vinci was actually there at the time –

PETER: Hmmm… no one knows anything do they…

PAUL: I'm pretty sure he wasn't there at the time.

PETER: You reckon?

PAUL: No, there was a big gap in when they were alive.

PETER: How do you know? You're only guessing. Was Mona Lisa there at the time? Eh? Was the Laughing Cavalier? There you go. What they all facing forward for anyway?

PAUL: Maybe on the actual day there was no table or it was a round table.

PETER: No, that's Excalibur. "A dream to some, a nightmare to others" – Merlin. Can't stand magicians. They have that air about them, you know, of the bullied child. They have to hurry up and pull something out of a hat before you twat them. Pitiful.

PAUL: Kids love 'em though.

PETER: This Tony and his bird, they got kids or what?

PAUL: They got a little baby. It can't be easy, you can't make a proper living I'm sure, she is like getting her work noticed but, bet they do struggle. It's not really the time now for artists.

PETER: Well, why be arsed then? No one's interested, there's enough paintings, enough music. We don't need anything new – fucking nail brush – we don't need them scratching round for something we haven't seen before. Our eyes have seen everything now, all the shapes...

(Wanders around his mind again.)

...there's nothing left for me to learn... there's only pleasure in picking at the sores, or giving them. Picking at sores or giving them... a vase is a painting is a cake is a song... is a scab –

(Checks himself.)

Just singing a song I know. You don't know it. Hmmm, he supports her, she's an artist – council renting?

PAUL: I don't know.

(Pause.)

(It audibly begins to rain outside. Peter looks at the umbrella and his mood subtly lightens.)

PETER: Ah well... no, he's doing his best isn't he? Trying to get on, get ahead – play the guitar – help the helpless and that... no, he's a good lad from what you said. You know what, I know you think I'm grumpy and though I am fun to be around, I moan a bit. But I don't mean anyone any harm. We're all after what's right, aren't we? Eh?

PAUL: Yeah, and helping people, it's a buzz isn't it? He gets a lot of great work and he's helping people do better.

PETER: Course he is, he's doing some good. I don't know how he does it.

PAUL: It must be challenging –

PETER: He's doing his best and you got to hand it to him –

PAUL: They're grafters.

PETER: Course they are. I'm the same, I've done loads of things that the powers that be would see as untoward on paper. With a kid, it's not easy, you do what you can. I'm not judging anyone who fiddles the system a little bit to get by with a family, no way.

(Peter seems to be adopting the kind of sympathetic charm he uses on his customers.)

PAUL: Me neither. It's like I said to him, if you declare your music money, it'll just mess you up. You know, with your benefits.

PETER: I've done that though, me and her, at first we had to. When the housing came to check up, we had to hide all my stuff next door. Great neighbours they were – understanding. We looked after each other. We looked after their dogs when they went away; they brought us back duty free. That's what neighbours do. I miss them more than I miss her. They both worked and they were an older couple like, their kids had left home before we moved there. They understood how we had to get by. I'll never forget that you know? Even though in the end they got involved in her side of it. You can't blame them for that. I know that when they seen me taking my stuff out to the car in bin bags, they knew she was in the wrong. Her crying in front of them... I've told you before anyway about that... I'm not going into it. But I've still got a lot of respect for the neighbours, for never shopping us in. An' I still let on to them when I pick the kids up... Tony and his misses... them two with a kid, she's an artist, bet they can't even tell them she does that...

PAUL: I don't know about that. I don't pry into those things me.

PETER: Hmmm... no why would you? You don't know that side yet, but you will, you get to a point and if you earn a certain amount you get all your benefits took off you and it is practically worse than the dole – fact that... that's what I'd do. Hands down.

PAUL: No one's losing out are they?

PETER: How d'you mean?

PAUL: What harm would it do?

PETER: None. No. You know what... I came in here all mithered and down and... I've cheered up now.

PAUL: We aim to please.

PETER: Yeah. All you've told me about him, it's really cheered me up. The person that he is and what he's doing, it's made me think about my life in a good way, that's the first time that's happened in years... So, you'll have a nice day tomorrow then?

PAUL: Hope so...

PETER: Eh and if you wanna pop the question, I've got a cracking ring. £150, worth about a grand.

PAUL: Bit early for that yet.

PETER: You know where I would go if I was you?

PAUL: Where?

PETER: I would get out of the city me and go to Heaton Park. The cherry trees, the lead lions, the boating lake, ice cream. Every kid in town's walked it there. I used to kiss girls in the rhododendrons. I'd hide in them and when a gang o' girls walked past I'd lunge out like a wolf, make them jump and then the one that was giggling I'd drag in with me. Yeah... I mean it's our Eden isn't it, or otherwise why would God send the Pope there? Yeah, I love that park. I remember going down the Ha-Ha Hill on a space hopper, right to the bottom – bouncing, leaping about like I was flying. You can have a paddle, play in the sand – it's paradise. Just like Eden, full of animals and things you're not meant to eat. It's just about having a good time.

PAUL: Thing is... I took her there in the summer. She got nipped by a Staffie. Don't think she'll want to go again.

PETER: Ah well. It's not like it used to be anyway. I should probably take my kids but they'd only want a balloon, next minute I'm carrying round a floating Tweetie Pie like a twat. Don't think I've ever took them... Oh course I did yeah, Bonfire Night, one of them pissed their pants at the fireworks, all down me shoulders. Ruined it for me... Home time for me, Paulio. Bacon fries please for the journey...

PAUL: Way ahead of you...

(Passes him the bacon fries he has had ready since the start. Paul takes the money and gives him the change, which Peter checks.)

PETER: See you next Friday then. Thanks for looking after me Paulio.

PAUL: No promblemo, Peteyboy!

PETER: What?

PAUL: See you next Friday...

PETER: That you will.

(He walks off into the audience then turns back, his breathing loud and felt and heard by all as he returns.)

Pouring down and an umbrella going to waste, we can't have that can we? He wouldn't want that would he? Tony Rabonni? I better take it, make the most of it and bring it back for him.

PAUL: No chance mate! You won't bring it back, I know you!

PETER: Course I will, I'm in every week, come on, it's lashing down and I've got no hood. I'll bring it back. He'll get it, trust me.

PAUL: Ahh, I don't know, I've kept it, he might come back out of the blue and –

PETER: Will he balls! Well, he might but... he doesn't need it as much as I do. He's got a little journey to get home, I've got miles.

PAUL: Ahh, Pete, don't take it though... I kept it for him coming back...

PETER: He's not coming back, but I am. Don't let me go out there without it.

PAUL: You better come back with it.

(Hands Peter the umbrella.)

PETER: Laters Paulio... *(Exiting.)* Have nice time tomorrow... oh hang on, didn't you say he has a gig tomorrow night? I'll take it for him.

PAUL: Yeah, he's playing at Night and Day.

PETER: Rabonni, brilliant, I might even film him you know, got some cracking cameras in at the minute, bet he'll appreciate that... see you when you serve me... again...

(He goes towards the door again, with the drums for 'Money for Nothing' building. The audience can feel him passing through and are helpless to stop him; frustration is enhanced by the building volume. Then, with the rush of the intro and right before the guitar riff, and as Peter goes to open the door to leave, lights snap out.)

MOVING PICTURES

24:7 Theatre Festival M.E.N. Theatre Award
Buxton Festival Best Comedy Award

"Witty, insightful and, yes, moving."
Manchester Evening News

Premiered at Studio Salford, 2004

Set in the ground floor flat of a house in Oldham, this play is about unconditional love for the family you know and the family that choose you.

Absent characters are heavily featured.

It is also a story of genetics, creativity, and bottoms.

CAST (2)

TINA

Aged 25+ and, initially, painfully self-conscious. A lonely, funny, combative, and ultimately beautiful person.

ANNE

Aged 35+ with impeccable comic timing. An annoying, loving, and beautiful person.

SCENE 1

Anne is laughing hysterically, holding her stomach, whilst Tina stands, shuffling awkwardly, trying to find a moment to speak.

Anne calms down and wipes her eyes. Then, as Tina tries to speak, Anne sets off laughing again.

This continues for a while until Tina quips in quickly during a moment of calm.

TINA: So, that was the bathroom, and this is the living room, obviously, it's quite airy and there is the gas fire but you –

ANNE: What did I knock off?

TINA: Oh it's just a picture, it's fine, I'm packing now anyway.

ANNE: It's not broke is it? *(Laughing.)* Should have told me there was a step there, I could have broke me neck.

TINA: Sorry, I should have said.

ANNE: Oh well I'm not interested now, I could break me bloody neck in here!

TINA: Well, okay.

ANNE: I'm only kidding – go on.

TINA: Right. This is the kitchen.

(Opens kitchen door and Anne pokes her head in.)

It's small.

ANNE: Mmmm, yeah. Everything's there though. Is that a dishwasher? You lazy cow! *(Laughs.)* I'm only kidding. Yeah, it's nice.

TINA: I'm taking the dishwasher.

ANNE: Oh, are you? Oh, I've got me own dishwasher anyway... me! *(Laughs.)*

TINA: And this is the bedroom.

(Points through to another area.)

ANNE: Lilac.

TINA: Right.

ANNE: Yes, it's alright that, very nice. What's that? Is that a tent?

TINA: It's a wardrobe.

ANNE: Oh. *(Laughs.)* It looks like a tent. Oh that's useful, does it collapse like a tent then?

TINA: I don't know, I've lost the instructions, they're in a draw somewhere.

ANNE: Yeah, you better have a look for them, you might have a problem getting it down and up otherwise. Don't leave it for me, I've got me own wardrobe, and I don't need a tent. *(Laughs.)*

TINA: It's a bit early to plan things yet.

ANNE: How d'you mean?

TINA: Well, you've only just looked at the place, you know –

ANNE: I love it though, I probably will have it, yeah.

TINA: Oh great, well, if you contact the agency –

ANNE: *(Sits down.)* Are you moving nearby?

TINA: Erm… no, I'm moving to Leeds and staying with friends for the time being.

ANNE: I could murder a brew if you're making one, the bus is ages yet.

TINA: Right.

ANNE: Coffee two sugars please love.

(Tina exits to the kitchen.)

Bet you'll miss it here, it's really nice.

TINA: *(Offstage.)* Yes I will.

ANNE: Is it warm in the winter?

TINA: Yes.

ANNE: Mine's not. D'you get a lot of junk mail?

TINA: No.

ANNE: I do, sick of it. I can't tell you how many times I've won a car. And a house. And a small cash prize. I don't mind the take-away leaflets, that's about it. Oh, and sometimes you get something about what's cheap at Lidl, that's alright.

TINA: Right.

ANNE: Sometimes something about someone's god. The worst is them that knock on, but I bet you don't get that here?

TINA: Er… no.

ANNE: Yeah, I had this bloke once, knocking on about did I want me suite cleaning. I said leave me something to read and I'll phone you. Anyway, I phoned the place and made some enquiries, fishing I was actually. I said 'Who's that bloke who came to see me, he looked familiar?' and the woman said 'D'you mean Dave with the red hair?'. I said 'Yes that was him, doesn't he live in Werneth?' She said 'No he lives on Maple Road, Chadderton.' I said 'Oh that's where I know him from, Maple Road, number 80.' She said 'No he's at 44, you're miles off.' I said 'Oh right, I don't know him.' Anyway, I banked it, you know, in me mind, and I said 'Oh, I'll get back to you on the settees.' And I thought right, teach you to come knocking on, mithering people. Went round when he was having his tea, I knocked on the window and pointed to the door. I said 'I've thought about it and no, I don't think I want me suite cleaning, but if I decide in the future, I'll come and knock on, alright?' I get sick of them, do you know what I mean?

(Tina comes in with the drinks.)

I mean, they should get a taste of their own medicine, shouldn't they?

TINA: Pardon?

ANNE: You haven't been listening to me have you? *(Laughs.)* Did you not hear me? *(Laughs.)* It dunt matter, I'm just rambling about door-to-door people, but I bet you don't get that here.

TINA: No.

ANNE: No, I won't miss where I am, I hate it. It's lovely round here.

TINA: Yes, it is nice.

ANNE: Oh, no, I hate it where I am. I've been broke into twice. First time, I blame meself really, left the backdoor unlocked when I went out and they took me DVD. Well, I didn't notice at first because I don't watch them a lot, was a couple of days after it happened actually. Well, it must have been, because I can trace it back to leaving the door unlocked, remembering and mithering all night, then I got back and thought everything was okay. Anyway, a couple of days later I was at me niece's having a look what she had. She said 'Lend this if you want, it's really good, if you haven't seen it.' Anyway, I looked at it and I said 'Sally Potter's Orlando? Oh no, I can't be doing with people showing off about their trips to Disney.' She said 'Don't be thick Aunty Anne.' Because she knew I'd read the book. I said 'No I'm only kidding, go on then, I'll watch it tonight.' Anyway, stupid me realised when I got in it wasn't there. Then I tracked it back to that night, you know, when I left the backdoor open. But they must have had a good look round before they took it. The twats came back a week later when I was out and emptied the fucking place. It was awful that. I felt like killing meself.

TINA: Oh, I'm sorry, did they find them?

ANNE: No, did they 'eck find him. I'm not bothered now anyway, they didn't take anything that meant anything to me, all my memories are up here. *(Taps head.)* You can't get sentimental over a bloody telly or money can you? I mean it's like jewellery, what does it mean? It's not the person. People don't buy it and think, 'When I die, they'll have this to remember me by' do they? They don't. But I just hate the house. Have you seen that advert where bacteria is in neon, you know, that woman cuts up a chicken and doesn't wash her hands and everywhere she touches you can see where the chicken bacteria is? Well, it's like that, he's everywhere in me house. *(Shudders.)* I think about them still being there you know, watching me, and seeing what new things I get. And some days when I'm in a bad mood I think 'Just fucking break in now, I'm right in the mood for you.' No, it's got too much, I need to leave; it's not good for me. But I'm not scared of them.

TINA: That's the best way to be isn't it?

ANNE: Have you ever been robbed? Bearing in mind, it could sway me decision on the flat. *(Laughs.)* I'm only kidding, go on.

TINA: No.

ANNE: That's alright then.

TINA: I did get mugged at a cash point.

ANNE: Oh I've had that. Twice. The first time… *(Laughs.)* I'm only kidding, go on.

TINA: Heh, yeah, no, they just ran up behind me and whipped the money out of the slot and carried on running.

ANNE: Did you do anything?

TINA: No, I just got some more money out.

ANNE: Oh.

TINA: I know I should have reported it but it's like you said, what can they do?

ANNE: No.

TINA: Pardon?

ANNE: No, I didn't say 'What can they do?'. I said they didn't find them. You should still report a robbery.

TINA: It was a few years ago now.

ANNE: Are you religious?

TINA: No.

ANNE: You strike me as a religious person, very forgiving.

TINA: Erm... I am quite tolerant, but no, I'm not religious, no.

ANNE: Mmmm. You do seem a bit.

TINA: My family are, but not me, I –

ANNE: No, I should be more tolerant I think. But so many things wind me up. I think I'll feel better when I move here. This is great for me.

TINA: Right.

ANNE: Don't you say 'right' a lot?

TINA: Do I? Sorry.

ANNE: What you sorry for? Stop being so tolerant you. Just tell me to shut up going on. *(Laughs.)* I never shut up me, I love the sound of me own voice. *(Laughs.)* Oh, I'm me own worst enemy me. I'm one of them that mithers you on holiday, you know, that you can't get rid of. I bet you're one of them that just wants to read aren't you?

TINA: Erm...

ANNE: Worst of it is, I know, but I just can't help meself. I just love people, you know, people are so interesting. It's like you with your – what is it you do? You did say, didn't you? Before? I can't remember now.

TINA: No.

ANNE: Didn't you say you worked at a hospice?

TINA: No.

ANNE: I don't know where I got that from.

(Long awkward pause whilst Anne thinks.)

Oh no, that was it! This woman on the bus coming, yeah, that's right, she works in the kitchen at a hospice, she loves it. I couldn't do it. There's something strange to me about that. Anyway, she seemed to be dead into it. Probably thinks she's doing some good, I don't know. Or maybe it's the money, I don't know. Probably is good money doing that.

TINA: Right.

ANNE: No, it wouldn't suit me that. I'm better around people who I know are going to be around for a bit. You know, get to know them. I mean working in a hospice, I bet it's like temp work, I bet. I bet you have to think to yourself, well, I'll keep me distance because tomorrow you might be gone. I suppose you could tell them things though, that you wouldn't tell anyone else. But would you want them to take your problems to the grave? Mmm. It's a toughy that. No, I'd don't think that would help them really, but they might want to talk to you about things that meant something to them maybe, other people wouldn't understand...

(Anne seems to be upset and springs up abruptly.)

Fucking hell, I better go. I'm gonna miss it.

(Anne grabs her bag and exits, running.)

(Tina sits dumbstruck for a moment but eventually goes to the kitchen, enters with some boxes and newspaper, and begins to pack things on and offstage.)

(Offstage there is a loud knock at the door. Tina slowly returns to the stage biting her nails. A loud knock is heard again and she reluctantly goes to answer the door.)

(Anne is heard offstage, laughing.)

ANNE: I can't believe that I've missed it, I think me watch has stopped.

TINA: Right.

ANNE: Sorry, but I can't hang about outside, it's starting to rain.

(Both re-enter.)

TINA: Right, it's no problem anyway.

ANNE: Have you got a watch?

TINA: I haven't at the moment.

ANNE: Where's your clock?

TINA: I haven't got a clock.

ANNE: You've not got a clock? How d'you smell? Awful!

TINA: Erm...

ANNE: Oh, no that's 'he's got no nose' int it, how does he smell? Oh just ignore me... Well, can you put the radio on, they usually tell you the time don't they?

TINA: Er... Yes.

(Tina goes to the stereo and puts on the radio – the station is playing 'Celebration' by Kool and the Gang.)

(Anne sits down and plonks her bag next to her, she seems a little agitated.)

(Tina sits on a chair and both women wait in silence for the end of the song to find out what the time is, but when the song stops another begins without the DJ's intervention.)

> **ANNE:** Oh, it dunt matter, I'll just leave to what I think is twenty minutes, they're every half hour, I know that. It's not my day today is it? Make a fool of meself me, I'm not normally that gormless you know, knocking stuff off and missing me bus, don't know where I'm up to today, I'm all over the place. *(Laughs.)* So, do live here on your own?
>
> **TINA:** Yes, I used to live with my boyfriend but it didn't work out, we're splitting the money on the flat.
>
> **ANNE:** Have you got any children?
>
> **TINA:** No, we did try for a while but, no.

(Pause.)

> Have you?
>
> **ANNE:** No.
>
> **TINA:** Are you my sister?
>
> **ANNE:** Yes.
>
> **TINA:** I thought, yes, I had an idea you were.
>
> **ANNE:** I don't even want a flat. Just wanted to meet you.

(Long pause.)

> **TINA:** What do you do?
>
> **ANNE:** What d'you mean?
>
> **TINA:** I mean for a living.
>
> **ANNE:** What d'you do? You don't have to tell me if you're scared.
>
> **TINA:** I'm not scared –
>
> **ANNE:** It's okay.
>
> **TINA:** Oh, thanks. I'm going to have a drink, do you want one?
>
> **ANNE:** No, I've got to go soon.
>
> **TINA:** Right.

(Tina exits to the kitchen whilst Anne now seems more relaxed.)

(Tina re-enters with what looks like a large spirit.)

Ask me whatever you want, I'm ready.

(Pause.)

ANNE: Are me Mum and Dad alive?

TINA: No.

(Pause whilst they both reflect on this.)

ANNE: Did they talk about me?

TINA: No.

ANNE: How did you know about me then?

TINA: Mum kept a baby picture hidden, the date on the back of it was a couple of years before I was born and had the name Annie written on the back so I asked around the family.

ANNE: Orphan Annie eh? Heh no, I'm just Anne, orphan Anne. *(Laughs.)* No, I'm only… kidding… who did you ask?

TINA: Aunty Barbara.

ANNE: I don't know who that is.

TINA: Mum's sister-in-law.

ANNE: Oh. No, I meant did you not ask your Mum and Dad about me?

TINA: This is a bit difficult for me.

ANNE: Oh, I'm sorry.

TINA: Well, you should understand, I can't be held responsible –

ANNE: Responsible –

TINA: I'm not to blame –

ANNE: Tina, I just wanted to meet you that's all, no one's to blame. I'm not holding a grudge.

TINA: I did ask, yes, I asked Mum and she said never to ask her again, I was only little, I think I was about seven. I was scared to mention it after that because she was very upset. See, so I'm sure it wasn't that she didn't think about –

ANNE: Well, we can only speculate about that now, can't we? I mean, I'm sure she thought about it every single day of her life. I would.

TINA: I think you should have phoned before coming.

ANNE: I thought you wouldn't see me.

TINA: Well, I should've been given the choice.

ANNE: Sorry.

TINA: I mean, obviously you didn't have a choice –

ANNE: Tina –

TINA: But that's not my fault –

ANNE: Tina –

TINA: I mean, I'm just a child, I was, have been, I was their child, I mean, I know you were as well, but –

ANNE: I'm not going to lay into you about this, that, and the other! I should have phoned, but I just wanted to do it on the sly. Now, that might seem unfair, but I don't care really, I just wanted to meet you, I mean, what's wrong with that, you know?

TINA: Because I might not have wanted to meet you, that's what.

ANNE: Well exactly. You probably wouldn't, but you have now. Anyway, if we'd have grown up together you wouldn't have had a choice, so it's like that isn't it.

TINA: No, it's nothing like that.

ANNE: No, it isn't.

TINA: You said you have a niece.

ANNE: Yes.

TINA: So you've got brothers and sisters?

ANNE: A brother your age.

TINA: You know I haven't a brother or sister don't you?

ANNE: Yes you have.

TINA: Apart from you I mean.

ANNE: So you're not religious then? *(Laughs.)*

TINA: No, not in the slightest. I suppose it's like when people work in a chocolate factory and they get so sick of the sight and smell of it they can't touch it.

ANNE: I was for a while. Well, I felt like I had to be, you know. Because my Mum and Dad, they told me as early as I can remember about... my – your – Mum and Dad, don't know what to call them really so, I felt like I had to be to sort of, be part of them, you know.

TINA: Right.

ANNE: But there was this one time, I had to take me son to church, it was part of him going to this school you see, we had to go to church and that, to get in with this school, it was the best in the area. So I took him this one day.

TINA: I thought you said you didn't have any children?

ANNE: Well, I'll tell you about that in a minute. Anyway, on this Sunday, there were loads of children there, it was something to do with the scouts and cubs marching, you know, when they go through the streets holding the banners up? Anyway, loads of kids were there and I thought, oh, it might be alright if kids go a lot, talking meself into it, so the vicar starts all these prayers and that. God it was boring, and they all knew them, I don't know how, probably from school, and me an' me son Joe was just sat there like a pair of lemons, I felt a bit sorry for him really, must have been a bit intimidating for him. Anyway, we were mumbling along, trying to join in. Then halfway through the vicar did this little talk. He said to all these kids, he said 'How much do you think you're worth, shout out how much you think you're worth', so, you know, a couple of them shouts this, that, and the other, and he's like 'Oh a tenner here, oh this girl's worth twenty, this lad here's worth five thousand and that', and the audience, well, parishioners what have you, are all laughing along and that. Then he goes 'Well, this is what God thinks you're worth.' And these two older scouts goes behind the altar where the vicar's standing and they hold up, and I'm not joking, they hold up this life-size Jesus on the cross. They're struggling with it and everything, and the vicar says 'God did this to his son to show you how much you're worth to him.' And what that said to me was if God could let his own son be tortured and humiliated like that, what is the chance of him giving a shit about my son? What that vicar said to me with that was God thinks you're worth nothing. I didn't take him again, and he didn't go to that school. Anyway, that was my brush with religion. I had to tell you that, because that bit there, there was important to me. It's nowt to do with you Tina, but your Dad training to be a vicar and giving me up, well that's like, it feels the same, and I can't tell them, but I'm not having a go.

TINA: So…

ANNE: I think I will have a drink now love.

TINA: Right.

(Tina exits and enters with a bottle of brandy, pours a glass for Anne, refills her own, then leaves the bottle on the table.)

ANNE: So what's happened to your boyfriend then?

TINA: What happened was we were together for a few years, bought this flat and drifted apart.

ANNE: That always seems a bit vague to me that, 'drifted apart'.

TINA: I suppose it's just a polite way of saying I had a hell of a time but don't want to discuss it, basically.

ANNE: Fair enough.

TINA: What happened with you?

ANNE: How d'you mean?

TINA: I mean with your partner?

ANNE: With me husband? Nothing, we're still together.

TINA: Oh, sorry, I just assumed what with the death –

ANNE: Oh no, I'm still married. It was hard, but we stayed together.

TINA: Are your parents still alive?

ANNE: Oh yeah, alive and well.

TINA: So, what made you want to –

ANNE: I was worried about you.

TINA: Me?

ANNE: Yes.

TINA: Why?

ANNE: I don't know really, but I was. I felt that you might be lonely.

TINA: But you weren't to know about, I mean, you said you didn't know –

ANNE: No, I didn't I just felt a bit worried, that's all.

TINA: I'm not lonely!

ANNE: Have you got some nice friends?

TINA: *(Bemused.)* They're okay. Have you got some nice friends?

ANNE: Yes. Have you got any brothers or sisters?

TINA: We've already established that.

ANNE: Oh yeah, I'm just a bit nervous. Don't know what to ask you.

TINA: Is this really necessary? Just phone me or something and maybe we can meet up some time.

ANNE: Well, I think I did something really brave, and I'm proud of meself for that. You wouldn't understand what it took for me to come here. But it took a hell of a lot of guts.

TINA: I'm just not in the mood for this. I don't want this right now. It's a shame that you couldn't contact your real parents but just, you know, move on. Just move on. I've got nothing for you, really, just leave it and go.

ANNE: You know you're some arrogant cow, you. Now I'm staying until my next bus comes. And call it scary if you want, but you're going to give me the time of day because I'm all you've got left.

TINA: Look, I'm sorry, but I'm not going to stumble through building some fake relationship with you. I mean, look, you've got to have some regard for other people's space and feelings if you're going to do something like this. I'm sorry it's not enough to bombard someone with blabber to excuse being so thoughtless and intrusive.

ANNE: Oh yeah, well it's better than being an uptight stiff bitch with a sterile flat and a sterile bloody life and probably bloody sterile in the bargain.

TINA: I am actually.

ANNE: Well I'm not fucking surprised. It would be hard to nurture anything with a body full of fucking sawdust. No wonder he left you. Probably sick of getting fucking splinters in his nob! I'm your sister! I turn up on your fucking doorstep, I wish I hadn't bothered now.

TINA: I don't know you!

ANNE: That's no reason to be such an ignorant bitch. It took a lot for me to do this you know!

TINA: Just leave.

ANNE: Well that's nice isn't it?

TINA: LEAVE.

ANNE: NO. Let's just calm down.

TINA: WILL YOU PLEASE LEAVE NOW!

ANNE: I WILL GO WHEN MY BUS IS DUE, JUST GIVE IT A FEW MINUTES WILL YOU!

TINA: GET OUT!

ANNE: CALM DOWN!

TINA: I'm not prepared to talk any further, I'm uncomfortable with your attitude towards me and you should understand that now and go. You're just making matters worse. Our parents are dead and there's nothing I can do about that, and they're not here to defend themselves which leaves me here with you on my own, and I've got enough shit to deal with. I've got enough shit to fucking deal with! I've enough on my plate right now...

(Whilst Tina is talking Anne takes her trousers down, shows Tina her arse and waggles it in front of her.)

(Tina stares in horror.)

ANNE: Stick that on your fucking plate!

(Anne struggles to pull her trousers up, grabs her coat and bag ready to storm out; she turns to see Tina weeping bitterly.)

Well, if things weren't awkward before, they sure are now.

TINA: You don't know why I'm crying.

ANNE: Oh I think I do.

TINA: It's just like mine.

ANNE: Eh?

TINA: Your bottom is just like mine. *(Crying.)* I hate my bottom and yours is just the same. What a ridiculous thing to do.

ANNE: I know, don't know why I did that. Anyway, it was nice meeting you, good luck with the move.

(Tina falls into a fit of hysterics as Anne goes to leave. She realises the situation and laughs along.)

'Tina knew the truth when she discovered how similar their arses were'. Sorry, I just couldn't think of anything else to do. Me husband'll say 'Did she look like you?' and I'll say 'There are certain similarities.' Mind you, a lot of people have the same arses... Oh, let's leave it now, let's not take anything away from the moment. Well, at least you'll remember me, maybe not me face, but still... I'm sorry you can't have children.

TINA: It's not as bad as losing a child.

ANNE: No, it isn't... Well, I don't think it's as bad anyway.

TINA: That must be the worst thing in the world.

ANNE: Oh, it is. Nothing feels the same again. I mean, you feel things but not really. You can't really drum up the same emotions you used to. It's very cruel.

TINA: When did he die?

ANNE: Ten years ago. We won't go into it. I can talk about feelings but I won't reminisce. I can't do that. I told you that church thing because that's important with like, regards to me and you, but I don't usually talk like that.

TINA: When I lost Mum and Dad it was five years ago, within a year of each other. And I do feel lonely and sad a lot. It's like I visited a landscape in my mind I'd never travelled along before and people can only understand if they've been there, on the journey. Is it like that?

ANNE: No… It's like… a different journey's begun that you have to trudge through forever. At first you're going there to look for them and after you realise you'll never find them, you've got to keep walking. You've got to go on even though they'll never know you haven't given up looking and it's pointless looking anyway, you just can't stop. It's like that.

TINA: Dad used to have some funny views on death.

ANNE: Did he?

TINA: Yes, well, you can imagine, a lot of his parishioners were old people. Well, most of them were old. There was this one woman who came to the church every day bang on eleven. And she used to pray out loud, in case God might be as deaf as her I suppose. And when she was leaving she would always say 'Bye Vicar, the next time you see me I'll be in a box at the front.' This went on for the next ten years. When she died the family had her cremated, funny that.

ANNE: Yes, did your Dad say anything?

TINA: No. Well, not to her family. But, he said, to me and Mum that he sort of became bored with waiting for her to die. *(Laughs.)*

ANNE: Yes, it's funny that.

TINA: No, I'm not laughing at that, I was just thinking about this thing that happened. Erm… this one time she was there and Dad was taping up a window, it was quite high and she didn't realise he was there. Anyway, as she knelt to sign herself before sitting in the pew, Dad noticed that she'd dropped her scarf. So Dad shouted to her 'Brenda', but she couldn't hear him, he said it several times until he eventually shouted 'BRENDA!' and Brenda looked up into the air and said 'Is that you God!' Well Dad was just thrilled by that and couldn't help but shout 'Yes Brenda, you've dropped your scarf!' And she said 'Where have I dropped it God?' And Dad said 'At the end of the pew my child!' And she said 'Oh thank you, I'll need that later, it's a bit nippy out.'

ANNE: Oh, that's lovely that. I bet he had a good sense of humour.

TINA: He did, he was funny. I miss him.

ANNE: My parents were bus drivers.

TINA: Both of them?

ANNE: Yes, it worked out quite well for them really, different shifts. Probably had the same views as your Mum and Dad I bet; that the general public are arseholes.

TINA: Yes.

ANNE: Moaners.

TINA: Yes. This was my Dad's.

(Tina points to a painting of a church on the wall.)

He painted it. It was their first parish after they were married.

ANNE: Oh right.

(Anne goes to look at it.)

Oh it's lovely that, idyllic. Eh, he was a good painter. Oh that's really nice that. I paint, not landscapes, well, I have done landscapes, but it's not really my thing.

TINA: Oh right, what do you paint then?

ANNE: People.

TINA: Like family portraits?

ANNE: Well, I have, sort of but not usually. No, I follow someone round for a week and then I paint them. Not like a stalker or anything, it's commissioned. Done it for a few years now. It's alright, yeah. You've got to give it about a week, let them relax into it, go with whatever they want, and I work on it from there. What you looking at me like that for?

TINA: No, I just didn't think you did something like that. That's really good.

ANNE: I know it sounds weird. Well, I enjoy it anyway. I don't make much, well… sometimes I do, but not usually. It depends what they want.

TINA: That's really interesting. I didn't imagine you did something like that. How did you get into that?

ANNE: Well, it was from going to university actually, and I took it up after that. I was dead into painting and I wanted to study more, so I did a fine art degree. You don't believe me, do you?

TINA: Why wouldn't I believe you?

ANNE: You're looking at me funny, like I'm lying.

TINA: No, I believe you, I'm just surprised. I just imagined you did something more, I don't know, industrious.

ANNE: Did you?

TINA: I just thought you did something more manual.

ANNE: Well, it is manual int it? Painting? I don't think you can get more industrious than painting. It's flamin' hard work. I think it is anyway. I mean, I enjoy it but it takes time. You've got to be like, really committed and that. I mean, I've done stuff that's took me ages, and I'm talking ages, to perfect, to get the right, well, atmosphere and that. Then one day I'll do the tiniest thing, and with portraits the smallest detail can change the perspective or like, the perception of the person – and that's it. It's ruined. And I start again and do it again, but it's never the same after that. That's the thing with being creative, you can create something you're not happy with, and it turns out wrong. That's me I suppose.

TINA: Right. It's great that, that you can do something like that, so creative.

ANNE: Oh well, I better get going.

TINA: Oh right. Well, shall we, I don't know, swap numbers or... well, you've got my number haven't you, so leave your number and I'll phone you or something, we'll keep in touch.

(Both stand.)

ANNE: You never said what you do?

(Pause.)

(They both look at each other and the atmosphere is awkward.)

Well, anyway, I'll give you me number, it's up to you now. So... good luck with the move and that –

TINA: Thanks –

ANNE: And it was nice to meet you, really nice. I know it was a bit awkward for you but thanks for tolerating me. *(Laughs.)* Anyway I'll – hang on have you got a pen?

TINA: Oh, right, erm... I don't think I've got a pen but –

ANNE: Hang on, I've got one I think…

(Anne rummages through her bag and produces a pen.)

Here you go! Just write your new address or, hang on… here's me number. *(Scribbling on a scrap of paper.)* This is my address and number. Just, well, whatever, it's up to you. I'm just glad to meet you. Sorry it's been a bit out of the blue… I'm happy, anyway, with the way it's gone. So… I mean, I don't know a lot about you… but…

TINA: I ran away from home when I was fifteen. I went to live with a man who was ten years older than me, not far, but far enough that they didn't know where I was. Had an amazing time chasing festivals and rainbows. I lost contact with my parents for a few years and squatted in various places, then I got tired of it and came home. I had a few temp jobs and made some friends and got sick of that and wanted to look for some permanent work so I could get a flat. I started at this insurance company and had an affair with the boss, he spent a lot of money on bedding me and I moved into management and then I became infatuated with the 'nice looking bloke in HR'. We dated for a short time then moved in together. Then my parents died. And I was grieving and that was too much for him. He spent a lot of time with work friends telling them how hard it was to cope with my grief, clung to someone who assured him she had shoulder to cry on, a settee to lie on, then regular sex to rely on. So that was that. Things change, we move on. Now I don't do anything. But I'm moving to somewhere else and I'm going to think about it and decide what makes me happy.

ANNE: Well, that's good that then, I hope you feel better. You've got me numbers and that. I'll see you soon… well I won't… but… just, you know… if you want to contact me you can. I'm sorry about what I said… about the sawdust and that. And I'm sorry that I go on, I just talk a lot when I'm nervous. It's funny really, me and you, we don't know each other, but we have this blood connection and whatever happens it's always going to be there. I like that, me. We're family now, really. I'm not bothered if you don't want to see me again. I don't know about you but I won't be upset, I'm happy with how it's gone. I mean, I know that we've only just met and that, but I'd break the limbs of anyone who upset you again. Don't be scared, I'm only kidding. But I'm happy just to have met you. I'm happy… that you're my sister.

That's enough for me. You're nicer than I thought you'd be. You're very beautiful. Eh, and I'm not just saying it because you're my sister. Fuck's sake, I better go, I'm gonna miss it again. I'll see you love.

(Anne gives Tina a kiss. They hug awkwardly and Anne runs out.)

(Tina sits for a while, reflects, then grabs her coat and umbrella, takes the painting from the wall and runs out after Anne.)

Premiered at Oldham Coliseum, 2007

Scenes switch between the dressing room of a pole dancing club and backstage at The Opera House in Manchester.

"Inspired by dressing, *Twirlies and Girlies* has four strong female character roles and is a play for two actors. Beverly and Tamsin are portrayed by one, Kim and Stacey by the other." *CC*

CAST (4)

BEVERLY

A performer at The Exotica Club. She's had enough. The pole has lost it's shine and no longer a novelty. It's become a tough job and she's jaded, to the point where she hates every punter and every man that works there. Beverly has a temper that she sometimes has no control over. But she doesn't want to hurt anyone, and hates having to say sorry afterwards. Kim is like the mum she never had, her safety net. If she's honest, she has only stayed at this job longer than she wanted to because she loves being around Kim. Beverly doesn't really enjoy her studies and wants to jack it in. She is industrious and knows there is something more out there for her. She hopes her jaded approach to men is short-lived, but until then is on a fierce journey of hate that takes no prisoners.

KIM

A performer at The Exotica Club. Kim is very comfortable and happy with her life. She is quick-witted and unphased by the things that happen; she's done it for a good long while. She is an amazing dancer and likes to make money and save up for all the best things in life. Soon she'll have enough money to do everything she wants. Kim is also a maternal soul. If she's honest, she has stayed at this job longer than expected because she loves being around Beverly. Kim loves all the make-up and costume of it all. She always looks amazing. She gives the best vibes and so receives them back.

STACEY

A chorus member in a musical at The Opera House. Stacey has missed out on many of the things young people do because she was in dancing and singing in shows and competitions from a very young age – her mum has pushed her at every turn. When her parents separated she was bereft of the love in stereo. Instead, it become something very hard to tune into, and the feeling of security and consideration dwindled. Stacey comes from a wealthy family, but one which didn't really understand the arts as a career. They were absolutely positive she would be a star as they couldn't believe her amazing talent, but once out in the world, Stacey realised that there was a wealth of talent and it was hard to be seen and to get work. But to her family she is and always will be the best. Her dad treats her like a child princess, her mum like a doll. Stacey knows that is a fantasy and the world is stark and not very nice. She is trying, but is now disillusioned, and this may be her last show. There are other things in life, she is sure of that.

TAMSIN

A chorus member in a musical at The Opera House. Tamsin comes from a long line of artsy people, a family with 'old money', and has parents who have the kind of wealth that means you have massive, freezing cold mansions that are difficult to maintain, but also plenty of property. Tamsin is in fierce competition with her sister, and she will eventually get to her sister's West End success because she is highly talented. She is kinder than she appears, but has always felt the cold, from family and from home. She thinks showing too much emotion is a weakness and leaves that on the stage where it belongs. This comes from a place of need; she needs friends so much that the feeling is almost unbearable to her and she absolutely cannot let the world see this in her, or she may crumble.

SCENE 1A

The dressing room of a pole dancing club.

BEVERLY: I can't concentrate on it tonight, that knobhead's getting on me nerves.

KIM: The one at the front table? I know, he's a mauler.

BEVERLY: Well I'm not having it, where's Mike anyway? He's supposed to be there all the time.

KIM: Where d'you think he is? At the top chatting up the bouncers again. Makes you feel dead safe doesn't it?

BEVERLY: Well I'm smacking him one if he touches me again. I don't care how wound up he is.

KIM: We had a wanker in the other day and Mike was nowhere to be seen as usual. Me and Fiona thought they were all going to be at it if they saw him. Like that Mexican wank we had that time, d'you remember? So we hung around him till he'd finished so the other punters didn't see what he was doing. You know that snotty cow barmaid? She told Mike we were egging him on!

BEVERLY: Everyone's too worried about losing their job in here. I'm telling you if he touches me again I'm going to dig me heel in his crotch.

SCENE 1B

Backstage at The Opera House.

Stacey has received a bunch of flowers and follows Tamsin around until she has no choice but to acknowledge them.

TAMSIN: Oh bless! Who from?

STACEY: My beautiful Dad...

TAMSIN: Oh, let me see... *(Reads.)* 'So proud of you honey, see you after the show, Dad, kiss-kiss-kiss.' Aaawwwwww.

STACEY: He's here on business this weekend. Couldn't make it last night, bogged down, you know? So he's taking me to dinner later. I've really missed him.

TAMSIN: Awww, sweet. I think Mum's coming next week, if she's back by then.

STACEY: Oh, where is she?

TAMSIN: Well somewhere in Brazil collecting some mad shrub that she doesn't know what it does but makes you feel wonderful. Actually I must get her to do some acupuncture on my back. She's sooooo good at that.

STACEY: Oh my god, does she do backs? Could she do mine?

TAMSIN: I didn't know you had a garden?

STACEY: Sorry?

TAMSIN: She does horticultural acupuncture.

STACEY: Oh right, no I don't have a garden. Does she do window boxes?

TAMSIN: No just lawns, if they're looking a bit barren, you know? She opens the meridians of the turf. Golf courses mostly. She's away a lot, Lanzarote, Catalunya, you know?

STACEY: Dad hardly ever gets chance to come and see me in anything nowadays, such long hours he does. I think he'll really enjoy the show though.

TAMSIN: D'you know that dresser is never in here. I mean, I actually need help buttoning some of these fucking bastard costumes up. Just because she's responsible for some of the minor principles, we shouldn't be neglected.

SCENE 2A

The dressing room of a pole dancing club.

BEVERLY: Yeah, he's responsible for us. We shouldn't have to deal with that. Is he out there?

KIM: I think he's gone to see Kev at the Opera House.

BEVERLY: For fuck's sake. Hanging round the Opera House bar and leaving us dealing with dickheads. I'm not going out until he comes back, I've had enough of it.

KIM: I'll go.

BEVERLY: No you won't. Supposed to be on a break.

KIM: I know but there's only Marie and Jane on the poles.

BEVERLY: Right I'll go. Just... try and get hold of him will you?

SCENE 2B

Backstage at The Opera House.

STACEY: I'm not waiting any longer, I'll have to try and fasten it myself. It's like you say, they're too busy sucking up to the minor characters to bother with us.

TAMSIN: Do you know I was under stage yesterday in need of a safety pin and I couldn't actually believe there wasn't any? My apron had come loose at the back and it was the crowd scene and you know how fucking quickly you have to get up there after the quick change. And I was worried that it would come off because I have to bloody run like mad from one side of the stage to the other. And there's a lot of bloody dancers in this show and if one of them had slipped on my apron I could have been responsible for ruining somebody's career and I just don't want that responsibility. Anyway I went to the quick change area demanding a safety pin and they were all chatting.

STACEY: Yes, I think I heard some of the dressers talking about that, you know. When I went for a ciggie.

TAMSIN: Did you?

STACEY: Well, I overheard one say to the other something like 'Who's going to notice her amongst the other plebs running across the stage anyway?' – I bet they were referring to you.

TAMSIN: It's funny what you overhear sometimes isn't it? The other day whilst I was signing in I overheard one of the crew commenting on somebody's saggy tits. Isn't that awful?

STACEY: Hmmm. Who was it? Just out of interest.

TAMSIN: Oh, I don't know, someone off the fly floor.

STACEY: Some men are so shallow.

TAMSIN: It's not the most important thing is it? People should concentrate on their jobs.

STACEY: No, there are far more important things. Like you said... about the safety pin situation.

TAMSIN: Hmmmm.

STACEY: Oh it's all drama isn't it? There's more drama off the stage than on it.

SCENE 3A

The dressing room of a pole dancing club.

BEVERLY: Don't panic, but I think I might have accidentally killed the mauler.

KIM: What?!

BEVERLY: Oh he's probably not dead.

KIM: What?!

BEVERLY: I said he might not be dead but... don't go out there.

KIM: What do you mean?

BEVERLY: Just don't go out there yet. Just, just let everyone calm down. What wigs have we got in here?

KIM: Why?

BEVERLY: Look, we're just going to have to go out there in disguise and sneak off. I'll wear that blue and silver one and you put the cowboy hat on and sunglasses. Get your stuff together.

KIM: Why am I involved?

BEVERLY: Because we don't want them to know which one of us might be me.

KIM: Who?

BEVERLY: Everyone's a bit annoyed. If they can't tell which one is me they might get confused and well, that'll buy us some time.

KIM: What've you done?

BEVERLY: It was an accident. He was mauling me, I'd had enough, I swung round on the pole and kicked him in the chest. He fell backwards and well it's looking like he might have had a heart attack.

KIM: Well did you check him over?

BEVERLY: No I didn't because I am not actually a nurse, I'm actually a pole dancer.

KIM: Where's Mike?

BEVERLY: WHO KNOWS?!

KIM: Someone'll have told the bouncers.

BEVERLY: The other girls legged it out the back. Whether they ran round to the front and told them I don't know.

(Banging heard and men's loud voices offstage.)

(Beverly phones.) He isn't answering.

KIM: Who is it?

(Offstage noise of group of men shouting aggressively.)

It's too late now. We'll just have to wait for the police. You'll have to say you did it by accident.

BEVERLY: They all saw me do it. They're witnesses aren't they? I'll just say it was self-defence. I won't go to prison will I?

KIM: I don't know.

BEVERLY: Will I go to prison?!

KIM: I don't know! How should I know?

(Lots of shouting and banging on dressing room door.)

BEVERLY: I don't believe this. Where's Mike?

KIM: What do you think Mike can do anyway? Look, the bouncers'll be down in a minute. Why don't you phone the bar? He's probably there talking to Kevin.

BEVERLY: Right. *(Phones.)* Hiya Kevin it's Beverly. What? The nurse's outfit. Ha ha, yeah, I know you do. Listen, it's not that important but is Mike there with you, I can't get through to him on his mobile? ... Hiya Mike it's Bev... oh your battery's low, right. Listen there's been a bit of a problem and we don't know where the bouncers are. They've gone where? To the pictures? Why? I know it's usually quiet on a Monday but what've they gone to the pictures for? To see a film, yeah that makes sense. Well, the thing is, one of the girls has accidentally, might have accidentally, killed a punter by accident. Erm... I don't know really because it wasn't me. Erm, thing is Mike, is that we're locked in the dressing room because his mates are a bit annoyed. Probably because one of the girls kicked him off his chair and he's dead I think.

KIM: HAVE ONE OF YOU DICKHEADS PHONED FOR AN AMBULANCE OR WHAT?

(Silence offstage.)

BEVERLY: Okay Mike, but can you hurry up please as we can't come out of the dressing room. Erm, no Mike, I don't think anyone is manning the poles at the moment, what with this happening and that. Okay then.

KIM: You know, they won't have phoned the police because they won't want to be a witness, will they? They won't want anyone to know they were here.

BEVERLY: RIGHT, WE'VE PHONED THE POLICE AND THEY'RE COMING TO GET STATEMENTS FROM YOU NOW.

(Silence offstage.)

KIM: Let's leave it a few minutes now. We better phone an ambulance.

SCENE 3B

Backstage at The Opera House.

STACEY: I can't get through to the stage doorman. I asked him to phone when Dad arrived and he didn't and now I'm wondering whether he knows to send him up to the dressing room. He's so miserable isn't he? Every show I'm like, 'Hi Kevin... bye Kevin' and he rarely looks up from the paper. I'm a person who can talk to people.

TAMSIN: I have a great laugh with the crew.

STACEY: Me too I'm always having a laugh with the crew, I understand their humour. He's just bloody miserable. Do you know the one thing he said to me? The one and only thing that man has said to me? 'Eh, I 'erd you was flashing yer tits backstage last night. I can get you a job at the Exotica bar if you like, me mate runs that. Just say the word.'

TAMSIN: My god, that was just like him. You're sooo good at regional accents.

STACEY: You know I can't do Northern Irish? It's the only accent I struggle with. But northern English, Manchester, Yorkshire, Liverpool, they're my strongest.

TAMSIN: I'm not bad at Liverpudlian actually.

STACEY: Go on.

TAMSIN: 'Can I have a pack o' ciggies please luv an' a under-arm deodorant?'

STACEY: That's excellent.

TAMSIN: My vocal teacher told me you should approach accents like music. Each one has a different melody.

STACEY: I can't understand why I haven't heard from Dad yet though, maybe he's lost, I don't think he knows how to get round to the stage door.

TAMSIN: Bear in mind it takes quite a while to clear the auditorium.

STACEY: I hope for god's sake they didn't stick him in The Gods. I looked at Front Circle where I was assured he would be, but I couldn't see him.

TAMSIN: Do you think he might not have made it?

STACEY: Oh, he wouldn't have missed it for the world. No, there was obviously a double booking on The Circle. If he couldn't make it, I would have been notified.

TAMSIN: Wasn't he meant to come at Christmas and he didn't make it?

STACEY: No, that was a mix up on my part. I thought he was coming to the Christmas eve matinee but he'd actually said New Year's Eve.

TAMSIN: Oh, I don't remember seeing him on New Year's Eve?

STACEY: No? Oh well, we just rushed off. He wanted me all to himself, he wasn't really in the mood for a party.

TAMSIN: That was a fucking good party. It was such a good atmosphere you know? When it just happens?

STACEY: I wasn't really in the mood for a party. It's all so superficial sometimes. Everyone's drunk and in love with each other but not really. Sometimes you just feel like having a peaceful quiet time reflecting on the year rather than pissing it away. Some special reflective time to yourself.

TAMSIN: But your father was there, wasn't he?

STACEY: Yes, yes, he was. Family time's very precious to me. Very precious. You're always the star in their eyes, aren't you?

TAMSIN: Not in my family love, my fucking bitch of a sister is in Wicked on Broadway. What does he look like, this elusive father?

STACEY: He's, I suppose, a bit podgy round the tummy, quite tall, red faced, bald mostly and what's left is grey. Blue eyes like mine. Always smiling. He's very confident, makes you feel well protected and looked after when you're with him. Mum doesn't really understand why I need him now. I suppose she thinks I should have grown out of him like she did. But no, still a Daddy's girl. 'One day,' he'd say to me when I was little, 'One day you will be adored by the world as much as I adore you princess.'

TAMSIN: Yes, I used to get that. They expect a lot from you don't they, families? Still, I'm sure he's still proud of you.

SCENE 4A

The dressing room of a pole dancing club.

KIM: D'you think I should go and check on him. It's very quiet.

BEVERLY: If you want.

KIM: I'm a bit scared, in case he's dead.

BEVERLY: Why, what's he gonna do if he's dead? I couldn't give a shit anyway.

KIM: I don't believe you, he could be in a mess.

BEVERLY: I don't care.

KIM: You what?

BEVERLY: He shouldn't go around thinking he can maul people. For fuck's sake he's old enough to be my Dad.

KIM: Oh put your burning bra back on, you work in a fucking pole dancing bar.

BEVERLY: Yeah, for the money.

KIM: Yeah, and that's what you do for the money.

BEVERLY: No, there's rules. Once I've got me degree you won't see me for dust. I am never working here again.

KIM: Right.

BEVERLY: That's if I'm not sent to prison. This is a wake up call for me.

KIM: Okay.

BEVERLY: Don't you think I'm serious?

KIM: Yes.

BEVERLY: You don't think I'm serious, do you?

KIM: Look, it's up to you, I'm not bothered. I'm gonna go and see if he's alright.

SCENE 4B

Backstage at The Opera House.

STACEY: Oh god, he's not moving. I can't get him moving. I think he's dead please help me, please. This can't be happening. This isn't real. If he's dead, I don't know what I'm going to do. I can't bear this. Please tell me everything will be okay please! Please! Please! Please tell me the next fucking line.

TAMSIN: It's 'I can't take this – I can't live without him – please.'

STACEY: Fuck. Okay. I can't take this! I can't live without him!

Please! Please! *(Collapses in a heap.)*

TAMSIN: Very good. Brilliant. So, when's the audition?

STACEY: Next Friday. I don't do telly very often so it's good experience you know.

TAMSIN: Hospital dramas are good aren't they? It's difficult to get anything long-running from them though.

STACEY: Well, my husband who I've accidentally impaled with a barbecue skewer during a dinner party is the brother of the canteen girl who is having an affair with the nurse who has recently been cleared of euthanasia. So it does look quite positive really.

TAMSIN: Well, that does sound promising actually. I'm going to have to get going I'm afraid. I mean, I'll hang on for a few minutes because I'd love to meet your Dad, but I must be in the pub for last orders or I'll miss my lift.

STACEY: Oh, you go. He's probably chatting and lost track of time. Silly man. No, you get going.

TAMSIN: Actually, I will hang around for a little while, I would like to finally meet him.

STACEY: You know, I'm wondering now, if I was meant to go and meet him somewhere and I've forgotten.

TAMSIN: Well, can't you phone him?

STACEY: Erm, well, I should think he'll have his phone turned off.

TAMSIN: It's worth a try, I mean you could be sat here all night.

STACEY: Okay then, I'll just try him.

SCENE 5A

The dressing room of a pole dancing club.

KIM: They've taken him to hospital. Mike's gone with him, he's not very pleased. Only because he's had to close though. He's alright, the bloke, he just banged his head, but with him being drunk he got a bit disorientated, that's all. Come on, it's alright. He's okay.

BEVERLY: *(Clearly affected by the news.)* I know but, it's like... you can't even... you feel like... oh you know what I mean. But there's barriers. And when they step over it that's when you feel what's going on. It scares you. I always thought, if anything, I'd be the one to get hurt not the other way around. I think I've got scared by me own strength in a way.

KIM: I know. Don't let it get to you. Here, have a free phone, it dropped out of his pocket when he was being carried out on a stretcher. Phone his wife up, that'll make you feel better.

BEVERLY: You get off. I just need a minute to calm down and that. Go on, see you tomorrow. I did care you know? I wouldn't wish that on anyone.

KIM: I know you did, see you later.

SCENE 5B

Backstage at The Opera House.

STACEY: There's no answer. I think I'll get ready and go and meet him at the front. I'm sure he'll be standing there wondering where I am. You go, I'm going to have a shower.

TAMSIN: Do you mind?

STACEY: No, don't be silly. I'll probably bring him to the pub. Unless he wants to whisk me off to dinner again.

TAMSIN: Well, tell him I said 'hi' and if we don't see you later we'll meet him another time.

STACEY: Sure. See you tomorrow babe, have a nice night.

TAMSIN: You too, bye babe.

STACEY: Bye babe.

(Tamsin exits.)

(Phones.) Where the hell are you? I'm in the dressing room waiting for you. I've been waiting all night for you, you've missed the show and my friend has gone and I'm all on my own.

BEVERLY: *(Picks up phone.)* Hello?

STACEY: Who is this?

BEVERLY: Who are you?

STACEY: Can you give my Dad his phone please?!

(Beverly puts down the phone.)

Paperboys is set solely in a pub in 2005. It's a tale of battling brothers, the complexities of family, and how time deceives the memory to create events which may not have occurred.

CAST (6)

RICHARD

Aged 60+ and Don's brother. He's chilled-out with weed, but also bitter and paranoid because of it.

DON

Aged 60+, Richard's brother and married to Vanessa. He appears kind, considerate, and a bit fuddy-duddy, but underneath is slimy, lecherous, and vindictive.

MARIE

Aged 25+, a nasty, bitter, insecure bully.

SAMANTHA

Aged 25+, clever and attractive, but a bit broken and old before her time.

VANESSA (aka V)

40+ and Don's wife. She's a bit like someone from *Dynasty*, if it had been set in North Manchester. A very voluptuous character, head matriarch in any situation, and keeps Don's balls in her handbag.

GREG

Aged 30+ and a drunk angel. He sometimes moves invisibly, and so knows everyone's story; a huge persona.

SCENE 1

Greg sits on stage mumbling and drinking whilst the audience arrive.

The cue for the play to begin is when Don enters and Greg exits.

Don sits bolt upright watching people and looking for the arrival of Richard. He has one pint for himself and one waiting for Richard.

Eventually Richard enters carrying two drinks, milling about, chatting to people, and looking for Don.

> **DON:** There he is, there's Richard. Here! Where's he bloody… I'm here! What's he doing the dozy… Richard you dozy…

(Richard spots Don.)

> **RICHARD:** There he is. Hey, I'm here!

> **DON:** I know, I've been shouting you for the past half hour. What you doing?

> **RICHARD:** Come here!

> **DON:** What're you on, you?

> **RICHARD:** Give us a kiss.

> **DON:** Don't be bloody daft, sit down.

(As Richard goes to hug and kiss Don, he swings the satchel he's carrying over the table and accidentally knocks over the two drinks Don has bought. He tries to put the two he is carrying down, but they also get knocked over in the stumble.)

> **DON:** You bloody idiot. Are you pissed you, or what?

> **RICHARD:** Oh look at this now, hang on I'll get someone to sort it out.

> **DON:** No, hang on a minute will you –

(Richard goes to the bar area, where someone comes to clean it up. He is as long as it takes to get another pint each for them.)

> Sorry about this love, sorry. It's him, he's a dozy bugger. I got him a drink, he got two, he's trying to give me a kiss and his bag swung round. I think he's already ten sheets. He isn't really, don't not serve him. He's just a bit, you know. We promise we won't be any more trouble.

> **RICHARD:** Who won't be?

> **DON:** Oh, here he is. Come on, sit down and behave yourself. Thanks love. Have you got anything for me wet pants? Cheers love.

RICHARD: Well I like to make an entrance.

DON: Yes Richard, well done. It's been eighteen months, how are you?

RICHARD: None too shabby, how are you?

DON: Fine, great. How's things?

RICHARD: Things are shipshape, officer.

DON: Well, that's alright then, that's alright.

RICHARD: Aye, d'you remember when you slipped outside the shops and knocked that old woman over?

DON: You what? What you bringing that up for?

RICHARD: I don't know, I just thought about it at the bar. I just remembered. It was funny that.

DON: Are you bloody daft you or what? Speak sense man!

RICHARD: Sorry, it was funny that, I just like reminiscing.

DON: Well, let's just get there in a normal way shall we? Jumping in with a story. Have you been smoking something? I'm not one of your giddy idiot pals you know? Just calm it down.

RICHARD: Alright Don, god you're getting old. You'll be moaning about your legs in a minute.

DON: Oh I'm going after this, what's the bloody point.

RICHARD: Anyway, how's it going? How's V?

DON: She's fine. She would've come, but she had something on.

RICHARD: Oh aye?

DON: Yeah, she wanted to come, but she had something on.

RICHARD: Oh, well. It's not her cup of tea in here anyway.

DON: No, but she did want to come.

RICHARD: Well, she dunt like bars does she?

DON: Oh, she does, she goes out occasionally. She likes a meal.

RICHARD: Oh aye?

DON: Yeah, she'd rather eat than have a drink. She said ask him to go for something to eat but –

RICHARD: No, I can't be doing with that.

DON: Well I know, I said, he's not going to want to eat is he?

RICHARD: I do eat.

DON: I know you bloody eat, I'm not saying that.

RICHARD: I eat at home. I like cooking me own food. You should come round for a meal, you and V.

DON: Well, I would, you know I would, but she gets a bit mithered round there. She dunt like leaving the car outside.

RICHARD: Well, come in a taxi.

DON: Oh no, she won't get a taxi.

RICHARD: Well get the bus.

DON: Oh no, she won't get the bus.

RICHARD: Well, I'll come for you.

DON: Oh no, she won't get in the car with anyone else driving but me.

RICHARD: Well, walk it then.

DON: What? Fifteen mile? Don't be daft.

RICHARD: Why don't you just come out with it? I know she dunt want to see me.

DON: She dunt want to see you again. Right?

RICHARD: Well, I'm very shocked and hurt.

DON: Oh I know you are, yeah.

RICHARD: I am Don, and you can tell her that an' all.

DON: Well, you shouldn't pick on her then. She's not made of stone you know.

RICHARD: Pick on her? She's at me every time. It's not me. All the years I've known her!

DON: Yeah well. She's still me wife.

(Pause.)

RICHARD: I'm having treatment, to see things more clearly.

DON: Oh, well that's... that's good then.

RICHARD: Yeah, well, I was a bit reluctant at first you know, because, well, they're in your space a bit with it.

DON: I bet it's worth it though. To get a better perspective on life.

RICHARD: Well, I wonder if it's a bit late in the day really. But they've assured me it works. I think it should be for younger blokes really. I mean, I've seen things like this practically all me life, you know.

DON: I know you have but... well, I think you're really brave. It's about time.

RICHARD: Yeah, apparently everything's sharper. More defined.

DON: Well, it will be, yeah.

RICHARD: You should have it done Don.

DON: Why should I have it done?

RICHARD: Well, you could do without your glasses couldn't you. Imagine that? They can work miracles now.

DON: Don't be bloody daft.

RICHARD: No, they do Don. They insert a lens in your eye.

DON: What for?

RICHARD: To help you see better.

DON: How do you mean, like rose-tinted or something?

RICHARD: Rose... what you on about?

DON: Well, what're you on about?

RICHARD: I'm on about corrective eye treatment, what you on about?

DON: I thought you meant a psychiatrist, you know, to get better.

RICHARD: Get better? What're you on about? There's nothing wrong with me.

DON: I know there's not!

RICHARD: Well, what d'you mean then!

DON: Nothing!

RICHARD: I don't know how you came to that Don. Why would you think that?

DON: Oh shut up Richard will you? I got mixed up.

RICHARD: Well, I think you should say sorry.

DON: You what?

RICHARD: Say sorry.

DON: What? It's you, you're always talking bits and pieces, it's hard to make sense of it half the time.

RICHARD: Right, it's me, yeah. I'm not very clear. Sorry about that. I'll try to be clearer.

DON: So, you going to Corfu this year?

RICHARD: Yes Donald. I will go to Corfu this year.

DON: When you going then?

RICHARD: I have chosen the eighteenth of the month of August.

Although if that is not possible due to flights or accommodation being unavailable for that time of the year I will think carefully about which date other than the 18th of the month of August I would prefer. Because I very much like the Greek island of Corfu and have enjoyed staying there for the past twelve summers of my life.

DON: Right, if you're going to be a dickhead all your life, I'm going home.

RICHARD: Okay Donald, thank you very much for having a drink with me.

DON: Oh behave your bloody self, you're like a kid half the time. You're your own worse bloody enemy and you wonder why I never bloody ring you.

RICHARD: No I don't. I know why you don't ring me.

DON: You what?

RICHARD: I know why you don't ring me. You don't ring me because you're so tight, that's why you don't ring.

DON: I'm not tight, you're just bloody selfish. You get yourself one of these mobiles and expect everyone else to fork out phoning you.

RICHARD: You could text me.

DON: Text you? Aye I'll text you alright. Text you, don't make me laugh. Have you heard yourself?

RICHARD: Come on Don, get yourself a mobile and we can have text with each other.

DON: I tell you, you're bloody funny you are. As if I'm going to sit there tapping away on a bloody mobile sending sex messages to you.

RICHARD: Sex messages?!

DON: I didn't mean that –

RICHARD: SEX MESSAGES?!

DON: You know what I meant! Oh carry on Richard, carry on, that's right you have a laugh, push me buttons, wind me up, you're good at that aren't you? That must be your talent that Richard, there you go, found something you're good at, at last, winding people up 'til they feel like lamping you.

RICHARD: Yeah, though I don't think it's a special talent that, more of a family trait.

DON: Had a postcard from Auntie Edie.

RICHARD: She didn't send me one.

DON: Well maybe she hasn't got your address, Richard.

RICHARD: I'm surprised she can still write.

DON: She's got beautiful handwriting, very elegant.

RICHARD: What did she have to say then?

DON: She said she was fine, and asked how you were and that she'd knitted you a jumper.

RICHARD: Christ.

DON: And she said she'd love to come for Christmas dinner.

RICHARD: Oh that's nice, you should be with your family at Christmas.

DON: Don't start Richard.

RICHARD: Well, you would've thought –

DON: Leave it Richard –

RICHARD: I mean you would think wouldn't you –

DON: I'm not entering into it with you, case closed.

RICHARD: It's the season to be jolly. It's called 'merry' Christmas.

DON: Well, she's not use to being that happy, you know that.

RICHARD: Well, she shouldn't have been that bloody greedy should she?

DON: She didn't know what she was doing, she was giggling like a bloody idiot. It's a wonder we had anything to eat, the turkey was like bloody granite, she thought it was a bloody sculpture. She felt totally humiliated after. You don't know what that was like, it wasn't funny – it was cruel.

RICHARD: I didn't know she'd have the lot of 'em did I?

DON: And d'you know Richard, she was made up when that came in the post. She really thought you'd done something kind.

RICHARD: So did I.

DON: When I got home she had 'em up on the tree. 'Look at these gingerbread stars, your Richard sent these,' she said. Absolutely made up, the ribbons on them and everything. 'There for us all to eat after dinner, isn't that thoughtful Don?' she says, made up she was. How d'you feel about that?

(Richard shrugs.)

RICHARD: I'd have felt a lot better if I'd have got to have one.

DON: Well, she'll not invite you again, so well done.

RICHARD: She'll come round.

DON: No, not with Philip's girlfriend being there.

RICHARD: Oh come off it Don, they're at University, do you not think they've had space cakes before.

DON: That's not the point. She wanted to make a good impression. Philip was upset.

RICHARD: He was having a laugh.

DON: No, Richard, you don't want to see your Mum like that. He was very upset. He was pestering Isabel to go up to his room all day.

RICHARD: Well, wouldn't you?

DON: Christ knows what she sees in him.

RICHARD: He's a nice lad.

DON: He is. He's lucky.

RICHARD: He is lucky, he could do a lot worse. Than you and V, I mean. A lot worse. It's a shame our Dad wasn't more like you.

DON: Oh, come on.

RICHARD: You're a great Dad, Don, he's a credit to you and V.

DON: Well, you know, do your best don't you?

RICHARD: Just goes to show, you don't need to rule with an iron fist to bring up kids.

DON: Well I never saw that side of him.

RICHARD: You did, you don't remember.

DON: Well, if I don't –

RICHARD: If you don't that's alright then. I do. I'd never treat a dog like that.

DON: Well, that's your side of it. I'd like to think I brought Philip up the same way we were brought up. Love and security.

RICHARD: Discipline and fear. That's what I remember.

DON: You were a cheeky bugger, still are.

RICHARD: I was a nice lad, quiet. You don't remember, you just remember what he said I was. That's fine, you respected him.

DON: You've never been quiet.

RICHARD: Someone had to stand up to him. Someone had to

help you –

DON: You were a pain at best.

RICHARD: I was armour. And the ammunition. An arsenal I was.

DON: Yeah, something like that.

RICHARD: That's funny for you.

DON: Arsehole more like.

RICHARD: Now, see, you've ruined it now overstating.

DON: I need a back.

(Goes into the audience to get a chair with a back on.)

RICHARD: Hey Don! D'you remember when you knocked that old lady over outside the shop?

DON: Oh we're back to that are we?

(During, Don returns with the chair.)

RICHARD: Skidding on the ice, d'you remember? Still cracks me up even now.

DON: Yes Richard, I remember, she was probably very badly hurt.

RICHARD: Oh it was funny that. Your papers all over the road, it was like a sea of papers.

DON: It was lucky for you that. You wouldn't have had my round if it wasn't for that.

RICHARD: Oh it was funny.

DON: If it wasn't for that –

RICHARD: It wasn't for that, you'd never have gone to grammar school would you?

DON: I wouldn't say that Richard, I think I wouldn've –

RICHARD: No, if I hadn't have taken over your round, you wouldn't have started having a good kip, and getting up after Dad left –

DON: No, if it wasn't for that, I wouldn't have lost me round and have had no bloody money to do anything and watched you out riding the bloody bike I was saving for.

RICHARD: Yeah well, you got a different bike didn't you?

DON: I didn't get a bike, you know that.

RICHARD: I wonder if I'd have gone to your school, if you hadn't fell.

DON: No, you wouldn't. I'd have still gone.

RICHARD: I don't think so. It was one or the other.

DON: How was it? It was a scholarship, it wasn't a choice between us. You had no interest. If you regret it now, it's a bit bloody late.

RICHARD: It's made no difference anyway. You're no better off than me.

DON: I never said I was! You know, you may as well still be ten, you're no different.

RICHARD: Not brain-wise anyway.

(A woman shouts from the audience.)

MARIE: Hiya Mister Ashcroft!

RICHARD: You mean me?

SAMANTHA: No, we mean Sir.

DON: Who is it?

MARIE: Me Sir!

SAMANTHA: No, me Sir!

DON: Who is it?

RICHARD: Move round for them Don.

DON: They don't want to sit with us Richard.

RICHARD: They do! Come on girls, I hope you've done your homework.

DON: Leave them alone Richard, they don't want to be sitting with their old teacher.

MARIE: We do, don't we Sam?

SAMANTHA: Yeah, course we do.

DON: You'll have to refresh me memory I'm afraid, what's your name?

MARIE: It's Marie Radcliffe.

SAMANTHA: I use to always wear trainers and you use to tell me off, remember? Samantha Church?

RICHARD: Oh yeah, do you remember Don, you always use to tell me about that lovely girl who wore the trainers?

DON: I don't think I did Richard.

RICHARD: He remembers you, I know I would.

DON: I – hang on, the Radcliffes – yes I do remember, there was five of you all told, yes. How are you doing Marie?

MARIE: I'm doing very well thanks. I'm training to be a nurse now.

DON: Very good. Well, I hope it works out for you.

MARIE: Thanks. Are you still teaching?

DON: Oh, no, it's not the same now, no, I got out of that about –

RICHARD: Can I get anyone a drink?

SAMANTHA: I'll have a brandy and coke please.

RICHARD: No you won't, you'll have half a lager misses, like the one you've got there.

SAMANTHA: No I won't, I'll buy me own fucking drink and have what I like.

RICHARD: Fair enough. Marie?

MARIE: No thanks.

DON: I'm okay, thank you, Richard.

RICHARD: Who's asking you?

SAMANTHA: Right, I'll have half a lager then. It's shit in here. Come on Marie, let's go now.

DON: Didn't you used to have brown hair?

SAMANTHA: Why, d'you remember me now?

DON: I think I do, yeah... You were a bit cheeky.

SAMANTHA: No, I wasn't. I was very quiet me.

MARIE: She was if you can believe it.

DON: I find that hard to believe.

SAMANTHA: Ah, well, there you go you see. Marie was the cheeky one, weren't you?

MARIE: I was a bit. But that's all.

SAMANTHA: And a bully, weren't you Marie?

MARIE: I wasn't a bully Sam.

SAMANTHA: You fucking were.

DON: D'you know I can't bear to hear a woman swear. It does you no favours whatsoever you know. Talking like that.

SAMANTHA: Oh does it not? Well that's me not getting a cake then –

MARIE: Sam, can you put to for some fags?

DON: Oh you don't smoke do you? Filthy habit that.

SAMANTHA: Give us two quid then.

(Samantha exits for cigarettes.)

DON: How's your brother Sean, Marie? I heard he became a chef?

MARIE: He did yeah, in the army.

DON: Lovely lad Sean.

MARIE: He is yeah, he's got two children now.

DON: Married then is he?

MARIE: No, he never sees 'em.

DON: Lovely lad, a brilliant boy, he really was.

MARIE: Everyone says that about him. I use to go out with Phil.

DON: Phil who?

MARIE: Your Phil.

DON: Did you? I never knew.

MARIE: I know, we kept it quiet.

DON: When was that then?

MARIE: A couple of years ago now.

DON: So... because he's...

MARIE: When he was in his first year at Uni, but then he went away.

DON: Oh... well...

MARIE: Sorry, for springing it on you, it was ages ago, it was just a bit of a laugh, I think he likes the older woman.

DON: Oh, well, Isobel... that's his girlfriend, is the same age.

MARIE: Isobel, I know yeah. She's really nice.

DON: You know her then, Isobel?

MARIE: I met her a couple of times, when I went to see him, she's nice.

DON: Yes, she's a lovely girl – you don't want to be bothering with bits of kids anyway, you!

MARIE: I know. I was a bit daft at the time. I had to end it when I saw how stupid it was. I loved your house though, that was a bit of an incentive, you know, 'all this could be yours one day' and that. Still, I'm seeing a doctor now so – quid's in!

DON: So, you've been to our house then?

MARIE: Yeah, when you was away a couple of times. I loved it. I didn't stay in your bed.

DON: Oh, good.

MARIE: No, I said to him 'No Phil, it's not fair that.' We had a big row over it... I didn't smoke in the house. Phil did.

DON: Philip doesn't smoke.

MARIE: Does he not? Oh well that's good, is he on a health kick now then? He needed it, believe me. He used to say 'Look, I get to do what I want here, me Mum and Dad are sound.' But I felt a bit awkward. I mean, you might be more free with your kids than I am, but, it's respectful, you know, when you stay somewhere.

(Richard enters with Samantha and the pub drunk Greg, all laughing and elevated.)

SAMANTHA: Eh, he reckons he's a pilot, don't you?

GREG: I fucking am a pilot.

RICHARD: Course you are mate.

GREG: You calling me a liar, you cheeky bastard?

RICHARD: No, no, if you say you're a pilot...

SAMANTHA: What kind of plane d'you fly then?

GREG: Fixed wing.

SAMANTHA: What's that mean?

RICHARD: What's that then?

GREG: Hang-glider.

SAMANTHA: Fucking hell, I though you meant you were a proper pilot.

GREG: I am, I've got a license.

SAMANTHA: Fuck off, that's like a paper aeroplane that you can hold onto.

GREG: Is it?

SAMANTHA: Yeah.

GREG: Oh, is it?

SAMANTHA: Yeah, it is.

GREG: Oh it is, is it?

SAMANTHA: Yeah it is.

GREG: Well, you know what? You're wrong. You're wrong.

RICHARD: These two are training to be nurses, Don. They might be looking after us one day. Imagine that.

SAMANTHA: Yeah, we could be wiping your arse one day Mr Ashcroft.

RICHARD: Chance'd be a fine thing.

DON: Yes, that would be great. I'd get me own back then.

SAMANTHA: I'd bring you a cake an' all if you were nice to me.

MARIE: D'you remember that thing he used to say Sam?

SAMANTHA: Are we keeping you up?

MARIE: No, that other thing. 'We're not here for the...' what was it Sam?

SAMANTHA: It was, hang on... 'We're not here for the ambulance.'

DON: Ambience.

SAMANTHA: Was it? Ambience? There goes my fucking illusions shattered. That's what made me want to be a nurse. I thought you were saying, 'We're not here for the ambulance.' Like, we're not here waiting to die. What did you mean then? Fucking hell, I'm having to reassess me whole life now.

MARIE: What you gonna do now?

SAMANTHA: I don't know, what fits with ambience?

RICHARD: Nice lighting, a bit of atmospheric music.

SAMANTHA: Doesn't sound like school to me.

DON: That was the point.

GREG: Some people find school ambient, like, it must be... You remember all the smells and sounds... coffee when it's cold we had, or the squeaking on the polished floor – 'Don't run lad!'

RICHARD: Yeah, some people loved school didn't they mate? Not me though.

DON: School was bloody hard in my day.

RICHARD: Course it was Donald. Still, I got the bike.

DON: It was bloody hard. It's a doddle now for the pupils, it's the teachers that have to work at it.

RICHARD: Oh don't start moaning now.

DON: Richard, the teachers are that tied up with paperwork –

RICHARD: Oh poor teachers –

DON: You've no idea Richard –

RICHARD: Oh I feel dead sorry for teachers me, god knows how many weeks off they have –

DON: Oh here we go –

RICHARD: And they moan. Moaning teachers, there's not one of them happy in their job. Makes you wonder what they do it for –

DON: Yes it does. It makes you wonder what the point is of –

RICHARD: I mean, why don't they try hod carrying, that's a hard job. Try being a fucking shop assistant Don –

DON: I'm not having a go at other people Richard –

RICHARD: Get back to us when you've fucking slogged for a living –

DON: I'm not saying it's the hardest job in the world, I'm just saying –

MARIE: Why don't you just let him get his point across, it's the same with nurses –

RICHARD: Oh, here we go, nurses, rushed off their feet. Doing what? Picking their arses and gossiping whilst the walking wounded sit around bleeding to death? They should advertise for work shy moaners the teaching and nursing profession, 'We welcome applications from fat-arsed sloths who can sit an exam but can't be bothered with a full day's graft.'

SAMANTHA: I bet you wanted to be a teacher you.

DON: He didn't.

SAMANTHA: I bet you wanted to be a teacher but you weren't clever enough.

DON: No, he did what he wanted.

RICHARD: I didn't want to be a flamin' teacher –

DON: He wouldn't have taught, he was a doer.

RICHARD: I still am.

DON: Very talented man our Richard –

RICHARD: If I wanted to be a teacher, I'd've been one, and a good one an' all.

DON: You would, you would've been very good.

RICHARD: I never wanted to teach. Having everyone sit down listening to me banging on.

SAMANTHA: What, like we're doing now.

RICHARD: There's more to life than preaching. More to be had than that. I had enough of that at home. No, I wouldn't have been a teacher in a million years. Thinking I knew better and well, deciding people's fate like that. On whether they can shut up and listen. No.

SAMANTHA: You don't listen to people.

DON: I'll get another I think Richard, before V comes for me, are you having one?

RICHARD: No Don, I've just got one.

DON: Right, well, I'll just get a half.

RICHARD: Get a bloody pint Don, what's up with yer?

DON: It's not worth the hassle Rich, she'll be reckoning on me being ratted, I can't be doing with it. Right then, alright, I'll get a pint.

(Exits.)

MARIE: Nice of him to ask us.

RICHARD: I tell you what, why don't you go and get him a drink.

MARIE: Why?

RICHARD: Why not? Why should he get you one?

MARIE: Because –

SAMANTHA: I'll tell you why, because he's retired and we're students.

RICHARD: Well go home then and do some fucking work for a change.

SAMANTHA: You know, you can't stand it that people get on in life and you didn't.

RICHARD: That's right.

SAMANTHA: You're a very bitter person.

RICHARD: I am.

SAMANTHA: You shouldn't be, that's wrong.

RICHARD: Okay then. I won't be.

SAMANTHA: Good, get us a drink then.

RICHARD: No, get your own or go home.

SAMANTHA: If I did, who would you talk to?

RICHARD: I would talk to my brother who I came to meet and who never asks for anything from me but love and security.

SAMANTHA: Well, I don't want that, I want a brandy and coke.

RICHARD: Well, that's all I got, so buy your own, you cheeky bitch.

GREG: A plane could tell you what happened, if it could talk. But the passengers, they couldn't. All their experiences would be different. But not the planes. And maybe the planes would be the most profound explanation, if it could speak or recount in some way. It's like the pen, the pen could tell you – or the paper – could tell you what's written, but not the writer, or the reader, their judgment's clouded. The table you sat at, at school, could tell you what you were like at school, but you couldn't, or the teacher couldn't, or your mates, their memories clouded. I've been passed the same tree as a man and boy in my street. That tree knows me better than I do and it's probably outlived three generations of my family. Have you got a fag love?

MARIE: Yeah mate, here you go.

GREG: Cheers darlin'. I've had enough me, you know?

MARIE: I know you have love, never mind, soon be morning.

GREG: It will yeah. Cheers darlin'. Thanks love. I'm harmless me y'know?

MARIE: I know you are.

GREG: I don't cause trouble and that me. I'm like a puppy.

MARIE: I know.

GREG: I'm like a little lamb me you know?

MARIE: I know you are.

SAMANTHA: BAAAAA!

GREG: He's gonna throw me out in a minute but I do no wrong me.

SAMANTHA: He's gonna baaa you in a minute!

GREG: Aye, he will, he does. But it's not on though. He doesn't know.

MARIE: No, I know.

GREG: He doesn't realise.

MARIE: He doesn't.

GREG: He doesn't realise I'm like a soothsayer. I can see me, d'you know what I mean? I mean I see things. These two, they're like this. *(Gestures weighing scales.)* The cunts are evening it up you know? It's Night of the Hunter. They don't know. Yet. They will. Night of the Hunter. One sees it, the other lives it. Who's to know. I'm fucking hammered me, sorry love, I don't mean to pester, I'm alright me. V'll do it. She takes it on the chin her. Why do the pub's shut at eleven? It's just warming up then. It's all wrong. The chippy near me is open at four and shuts at seven, but then from Thursday until Saturday, no, well, it would be Sunday morning then, it opens 'til twelve. I don't mean mid-morning, not noon Sunday, I mean Sunday no, Saturday midnight, Sunday morning. It's all one big adventure. Life. I'm having a great time. I'll just be over here if you need me.

MARIE: Okay then, see you later.

SAMANTHA: What? What did it say?

MARIE: I don't know, I'm just agreeing with him.

SAMANTHA: Hey, Red Baron, stop mithering us.

DON: The Red Baron eh? Eric von –

RICHARD: Von Richtove, the Red Baron.

DON: Didn't he have a bi-plane?

GREG: Tri-plane. They thought at the time more wings were better –

SAMANTHA: Shut up.

GREG: You what? Who are you, don't you tell me to shut up, you're on the side line, you're the chorus love –

SAMANTHA: Will you stop jibbing in knobhead?

RICHARD: Why don't you sit and listen, you might just learn something you should've picked up in school.

SAMANTHA: Eh you, I did very well in school actually, don't talk to me like a piece of shit –

RICHARD: Fine lot of good it did you, arsed about for years, now you're studying nursing,

SAMANTHA: Biochemistry actually.

RICHARD: Bio – yeah, I bet you can't even bloody spell it –

SAMANTHA: I do have trouble spelling actually, made loads of mistakes in me last paper on proteomics, still me theories were apparently groundbreaking –

DON: Really? Bloody hell...

SAMANTHA: No, not really, but I could do that for all he knows knobhead. Anyway, let me guess, you grow and sell your own organic tomatoes?

RICHARD: No.

MARIE: Onions?

RICHARD: No.

SAMANTHA: Vegetarian café in Stockport?

RICHARD: No.

MARIE: Withington?

RICHARD: No.

DON: He's a car salesman.

SAMANTHA: Is he 'eck!

MARIE: Are you?

DON: His own showroom and everything.

MARIE: Are you?

SAMANTHA: Is he 'eck!

DON: Oh, he is. He's done very well for himself our Richard, very well.

RICHARD: Just goes to show, you don't need to have a degree to get on in life.

DON: It does Richard, yes. I think it shows it's the person, and not the qualification.

RICHARD: It's hard bloody grafting –

DON: It is Richard –

RICHARD: You can sit on your arse all day reading or you can get out there and earn your crust.

DON: Very true.

RICHARD: Teaching's no graft –

DON: Richard –

RICHARD: I mean, where does it get you Don really? It's a fucking waste.

(V enters.)

V: Don, I'm here now.

(V exits.)

DON: Righty oh, I'll see you soon Richard.

RICHARD: Yeah, see you Don, see you V.

(Don exits.)

MARIE: Shall we get a bottle of wine between us?

SAMANTHA: Yeah, eyar.

MARIE: D'you want a glass?

RICHARD: Aye, go on then, here.

MARIE: No, it's alright, we'll get it.

RICHARD: If you insist, I won't argue.

SAMANTHA: Yeah, it's alright.

(Marie exits.)

Is that his wife?

RICHARD: Yeah, Vanessa.

SAMANTHA: Is she a teacher as well?

RICHARD: No. I think she works in a bank now. She's done all sorts.

SAMANTHA: How does she put up with him?

RICHARD: Oh, he's alright, he does no harm. He's great with her and Phil.

SAMANTHA: Yeah, but – he's a bit of a lech though.

RICHARD: Our Don? Is he hell. He wouldn't know where to start.

SAMANTHA: He is.

RICHARD: No, you're wrong there, love.

SAMANTHA: He was at school, not with us, but he was.

RICHARD: I think you might have the wrong teacher there love. Our Don, he isn't that sort of person.

SAMANTHA: I'm not being funny, but it was well known at our school.

RICHARD: No, you must have got him mixed-up –

SAMANTHA: No, I haven't. Or what am I saying here now, but I don't want you to think I'm lying, it was him, Mr Ashcroft, he had this thing about this girl in the fifth year –

RICHARD: I'm telling you, you've made a mistake, it's definitely not Don, he wouldn't dream of something like that.

SAMANTHA: Well, that's what everyone used to say. He used to buy her a cake at dinnertime and everyone said it was because something was going on. He was dead obvious about it, I'm not joking, he did. I remember seeing it meself, I'm not just making it up.

RICHARD: I'm telling you, you'll have got it wrong.

SAMANTHA: I'm sorry but, I'm not trying to upset you, I know he's your brother and that, I'm just telling you what we all say and what everyone said. It might have been something else, some reason he did it, but he was always hanging round her.

(Marie enters.)

Am I right Marie, about Mr Ashcroft, when he used to buy that girl in the fifth year cakes. What was her name?

MARIE: I can't remember her name, but yes, he did use to buy her cakes. It was a bit weird.

SAMANTHA: Oh come on, I've told him what everyone used to say.

MARIE: I never said owt to Phil.

SAMANTHA: Well, you're not gonna do are you?

RICHARD: Phil, Phil who?

SAMANTHA: She was seeing Phil Ashcroft.

RICHARD: Philip? What, you were?

MARIE: Why?

RICHARD: When?

MARIE: A couple of years ago.

RICHARD: How old are you?

MARIE: Thirty-six.

RICHARD: Philip is twenty-one now.

MARIE: So?

RICHARD: He's half your age!

MARIE: No he isn't! Anyway, I don't look that much older than him.

RICHARD: You do! What was he thinking!

MARIE: Actually, we were very close. I was gutted when we broke up.

RICHARD: Yeah, course you were! Nineteen?!

MARIE: It wasn't like that.

SAMANTHA: Anyway, Mr Ashcroft can't say owt, not after what he was up to.

RICHARD: No, you're wrong about that, Donald would never do anything like that, and I'll tell you something else, him and V would've been very upset if they'd've known about you.

MARIE: Well, it's all over now.

RICHARD: Nineteen. If I'd've been knocking around with a nineteen-year-old at thirty-four, I wonder how that would've gone down?

SAMANTHA: You what? You'd do it now if you could.

RICHARD: Course I would, but it just goes to show, double standards.

SAMANTHA: I bet you do it now, cruising around the six forms with your flash car.

RICHARD: Don't be daft. I don't have a car anyway, I have a bike me. I don't like cars that much.

MARIE: What d'you sell them for then?

RICHARD: Because other people do.

MARIE: You're not going to say anything are you? To Mr Ashcroft?

RICHARD: No, I'm not, because I know you've either got the wrong person, or there's something, some reason behind it, not what it seemed like. He's a lovely man Don, he's not like that.

GREG: Things that travel and that, they're so important and like grand, they can outlive the journey but sometimes people can't and that. I love gliding me, I feel like I'm more in charge and that. But I'm not. I could die in flight and the wings would just, like carry me. Like an angel.

RICHARD: Yes, Not a nice thought though is it?

GREG: A corpse flying about, maybe for ages. Maybe for days – whoosh! Dead, journey of a lifetime. That's what happens. People, they're flying round dead or unconscious, they started the journey off taking everything in and then they just die, but the wings are carrying them, the wings of the past and they don't know.

SAMANTHA: Will you shut it you, you're doing me head in now.

MARIE: I'd like to go back in time and freeze myself at fifteen, I loved fifteen me. I was beautiful.

SAMANTHA: You thought you were.

MARIE: Well, that's the same though, because when you think you're something, you are.

SAMANTHA: You were horrible.

MARIE: No I wasn't.

SAMANTHA: You were always picking on me, you were a bully.

MARIE: I don't even remember you at school, you were just dead quiet.

SAMANTHA: Yeah, I was quiet, that's why you picked on me.

MARIE: I don't even remember saying two words to you Sam, in the whole five years.

(V re-enters followed by Don.)

V: Have you got a problem with Don going Richard? It is alright isn't it? Because I wouldn't want to upset you or anything.

RICHARD: Yes V, it's fine.

V: Because, of course, the last thing I'd want to do is make you upset Richard. I'm very very sorry to upset you Richard and make you feel bad. I only want you to feel happy and nice and relaxed and confident –

DON: Will you just leave it V –

RICHARD: Don't worry V, I do feel relaxed and confident and happy and nice.

V: Oh well, that's good then. Because I can come and get Don any time I like.

RICHARD: Of course you can V. Is that your keys jangling in your handbag or Don's testicles.

DON: Richard –

V: You're right, it's Don's testicles, Richard. Right where I like them. And let me tell you something, it's right where Don wants them as well, because having his nuts in my handbag makes him feel very happy indeed!

RICHARD: I'm sure it does love. It must do because you shout him and he goes running and screaming like a woman.

V: Oh does he now?. Screaming like a woman, you mean like this – AAAAAAAAAAAAAAAHHHHHHHHHHHHH!

(An incredible guttural roar comes from V into Richard's face. Greg, Samantha and Marie laugh uncontrollably.)

That's how a woman screams Richard, when she's been totally humiliated, she screams like that inside. Not whingeing and whining like you do. Sneering and cackling like a bloody hyena that can't get a scrap. Whingeing about you being a paperboy, you child. Is that why you humiliated me in front of my son? Because you didn't go to fucking grammar school, you infant! You made me look ridiculous in front of my son, the one person in this family that shows me respect –

DON: Now V, that's not true.

V: Oh be quiet Don, I'm not on about you. You deliberately ruined that day because you are that fucking jealous of Don and me. And you would think that having never, never come for Christmas dinner that you would be have been honoured –

RICHARD: Honoured?

V: I don't mean honoured I mean, grateful –

RICHARD: Grateful?

V: Yes, grateful you sad bastard! Because otherwise you'd be spending it on your own like you always do.

RICHARD: I should be grateful that me only brother, me only family, invited us round for Christmas.

DON: I always invite you –

V: We always invite you, but the only time you came was when you'd cooked up some scheme to humiliate me. And there's me thinking we'd turned a corner. You're nothing but a self-obsessed child, a silly boy.

RICHARD: Right well that's settled, then. Okay then let's all sit down and have a drink together, shall we? Have a lovely sit down and a drink and all be okay. We sigh a huge sigh of relief, relax and enjoy the ambulance. Shall we girls? Isn't that right?

V: I've got nothing more to say to you –

RICHARD: Good, because I've got something to say, and you'll listen to me. I sacrificed a lot for that kid, I got up early and went to bed late, took the drunken beatings at night and the hangover beatings in the morning. And for years the most I ever got to read was them fucking tattoos. Love, hate. He says to me, 'On the one hand there's love, on the other there's hate, and they're always grappling with each other lad, to see who wins me over.'

V: Well, I'm going to tell you something that Richard never could –

DON: No –

V: That was from a film you went to watch, Night of the Hunter. It's Bob Mitchum that said that, not your Dad.

SAMANTHA: Oh god, yeah it is, yeah Night of the Hunter, with Shelly Winters and Bob Mitchum, does that with his hands. And he's really cruel to his kids and Shelly Winters, was it Shelley Winters?

V: I don't know, I think so.

SAMANTHA: You look lovely by the way, very nice.

V: Oh, thank you, I've been out for a meal.

DON: Dad didn't have any tattoos Rich, I've got photos I can show you, he didn't. So, it's like, you might have got it wrong, I don't remember him being as bad as all that.

RICHARD: No, I haven't got it wrong, I know how he made me feel, otherwise, I wouldn't feel like this. Why, if it wasn't like that, do I feel so terrible about him?

DON: Well, because you idolised him.

RICHARD: He beat me.

DON: Once he did, yeah, from what I remember, and it was pretty bad. I can't remember what you'd done now, I think you'd been stealing from the jar. But it was hard for him, I don't know any men bringing up kids on their own even now. It was hard.

RICHARD: No Don, you mustn't make out that me Dad wasn't cruel to us. I know I might have got the tattoo wrong but you've got to trust what I say. I took a lot so you didn't have to. You might find that hard to accept, but that's the truth that.

DON: I just can't remember that. What I remember is us being mainly happy. You in a lot of ways, from what I remember, were closer to him than me and you were absolutely heart broken when he died and you never talk about that Richard, you only ever talk in an angry sense about him. I think you felt you'd let him down –

RICHARD: Piss off! Why would I think that? Because I sodded off to Uni and never brought a penny into the house? Is that what I did?

DON: I'm trying to understand why you feel like this, why you've never talked about how upset you were at the time.

RICHARD: I was upset because he was me Dad. And I don't like talking about that because… because he was a bastard. You don't know, you can't remember.

V: Don has a very good memory Richard, he never needs a list.

DON: Oh be quiet V will you? You can put the bloody can opener down now, the worms are out already.

RICHARD: I'd have gone for the wooden spoon meself.

DON: It's just stupid to constantly put this between us. It's never going to be resolved is it?

RICHARD: People remember what they choose to remember, I know that, and I'm sorry for, I shouldn't keep on at you with it, it's not your fault – you two should learn from that shouldn't you? With your daft story about that girl. I'll go and get you and V a drink, pint Don?

DON: Go on then.

V: I'll just have a brandy and coke please.

(Richard exits.)

DON: This is my wife Vanessa, and this is Marie and Sandy.

SAMANTHA: Samantha.

DON: Sorry love, there's so many of you, you know.

SAMANTHA: You remembered her though. Must have been one of your favourites.

DON: Oh, I never had favourites me.

SAMANTHA: Yeah right, I bet you used to buy her cakes an all, no wonder Phil fancied her.

MARIE: Shut up Sam –

V: What's that?

SAMANTHA: Well, we never saw it personally or you might've done, didn't you? But the rumour at school was that Mr Ashcroft used to buy this girl in the fifth cakes at dinner time because she was doing a bit with him. Oh, you know what school gossip's like.

MARIE: It was just a stupid rumour that's all.

V: Oh know it wasn't. Don did used to buy cakes for one of his pupils didn't you Don?

DON: Yes, I did.

V: What was her name now?

DON: She was called Grace Hughes.

SAMANTHA: Oh yeah, that was it wa'n't it, Marie. Grace Hughes.

V: Grace, yes, such a lovely girl. We were both very fond of her. I hope she's okay.

DON: She will be.

SAMANTHA: You met her then, did you?

V: Don used to give her extra English lessons to catch up because she'd had some time off to have a baby, but she was so bright, and so eager to do well, Don convinced her to come back to school. She was very brave to do what she did, her family weren't very supportive were they Don? Don often visited her whilst she was off, to see how she wasn't getting on. It was me actually that said to Don, get that girl back in school and help her to do well.

DON: I said to her, every time you get a good result, I'll buy you a cake at lunchtime.

V: That's right, and she did very well. I hope she's alright. She moved away after school, didn't she Don. Her family moved to New Zealand. But Don had done right by her, he got her through her exams. She sent him pictures for a bit of her little boy Harry, cute little thing he was. She even invited Don over to see her, but we didn't think that was appropriate really, it was time for her to move on, get on with her new life.

DON: So you see, you shouldn't jump to conclusions should you?

SAMANTHA: Well, it just goes to show there are nice people in the world. Int that nice Marie, Grace has a little boy called Harry.

MARIE: I used to go out with Phil. Your Phil.

V: Did you? Oh. Marie, oh yes, I think, he did mention a Marie.

MARIE: Yeah, it was a couple of years ago now, when he started Uni.

V: Yes, I remember him mentioning you.

MARIE: We stayed at your house a couple of times, when you were on holiday.

V: Did you?

MARIE: We didn't stay in your bed or anything.

V: He's had that many girlfriends but yes, I remember a Marie, he said you were... older.

MARIE: It never bothered him, I don't think he noticed actually. Nobody else did, with him being fat, he looked older anyway.

SAMANTHA: You get that a lot don't you, fat lads with older women?

V: He was a bit chunky wasn't he. He's not now though, maybe that's we he has a lovely girlfriend of the same age now. Isobel, beautiful girl she is.

MARIE: Yes I know Isobel, she is lovely.

V: Lovely girl, very clever, got her head screwed on.

MARIE: That's good upbringing that, you can see it I think. I wasn't as lucky as what's-her-name though, Grace, no one gave a toss what I did. Just one of the Radcliffes me. Everyone thought Sean was the one with brains, now he's gone off the rails and I'm studying to be a nurse and seeing a doctor. She's learnt by my mistakes.

(Richard returns with the drinks.)

RICHARD: Here we are, try not to knock 'em over Don.

DON: I didn't knock 'em over, it's you with your bloody schoolbag. What you carrying that around for anyway?

RICHARD: Oh sorry, got it wrong again have I?

V: He likes baggage, don't you Richard?

RICHARD: I do V, I thrive on it. Not happy unless I'm moaning about something. Moaning, something you know a lot about from what I remember.

DON: You're not starting on her again are you?

RICHARD: Oh no, I wouldn't dream of it.

V: Don't upset yourself Don, he wants that. He doesn't bother me, I just ignore his little jibs.

DON: You're a bit bloody dressed up aren't you?

V: No I'm not! I've been out for a meal.

DON: Who with? Diane?

V: Yes, that's all.

SAMANTHA: You do look very nice.

DON: Where've you been?

V: The Simla.

DON: The Simla where?

V: Where it always is, near us.

DON: Bit dressy for that?

SAMANTHA: For god's sake, why, where d'you think she's been?

V: I know, where d'you think I've been, honest to god.

SAMANTHA: You're very lucky you, I bet she thinks she's picked the wrong brother sometimes.

V: I do not!

DON: Aye, I bet she does an' all, bloody hell.

RICHARD: Oh no, she won't think that, that's for sure.

V: I don't!

MARIE: Yeah, she's picked the right brother, he's very much like Phil, I can see that.

V: I'm not bothered love. None of us are. We don't care if you've been out with Philip or slept in our bed, or smoked in our house. That's fine. Because Philip will make the right decisions in the end. It was just a silly little fling.

MARIE: Was it?

V: Yes, it was. A pointless, frivolous, bit of nothing.

MARIE: Yeah, it was, and I'm with a doctor now.

V: Good for you, well done.

SAMANTHA: She's only got a bit dressed up to show off to your brother, for fuck's sake, deal with it. It's just a bit of a, you know, bit of a thing, to say – look at me, this is what you're missing.

GREG: I think I need to go in a minute, I've had my fill. What's that song... I love it, what's, how's it go now, oh, it's dead good, you'll know it...

V: I've been for a meal Don, that's all.

RICHARD: I think I will come this Christmas.

DON: Who the fuck asked you to come?

SAMANTHA: Don't swear.

DON: Will you just piss off back to that table you came from?

MARIE: Sam, just shut up.

SAMANTHA: Why, gonna flush me head down the toilet are you?

MARIE: I feel like it, yeah.

SAMANTHA: Well, those days are over. Going home crying, having no friends. Why? Because I was quiet and let you all say what you wanted about me? Making insinuations about me. Ah, but I'm not a pushover any more, me.

MARIE: You're still weak.

SAMANTHA: What?

(From this point until Greg begins 'I'm a little angel me...', the dialogue between Marie and Samantha and Don, V and Richard is spoken at the same time, sometimes audible, often overlapping. Interesting snippets that are intended to make the audience hungry for the little stories they get a glimpse of.)

MARIE: She gets like this sometimes. She'll be sorry in the morning.

SAMANTHA: I think we'll go and sit back down there now. Come on Marie.

MARIE: No.

SAMANTHA: Come on.

MARIE: No, I'm staying here now, see ya.

SAMANTHA: I'm not sitting on me own.

MARIE: Go then.

SAMANTHA: I can't go on me own.

MARIE: Well, you'll have to sit and wait for me then won't you?

SAMANTHA: Why you being like this?

MARIE: I'm just trying to calm you down Sam, you've gone over the top, you've shown me up, that's all. You make me wonder why I came out with you. I've got better things to do than spend the night with you showing yourself up. Fine, you've took me out, and I appreciate it but, you're gonna have to sort yourself out if you want me to come out with you again.

SAMANTHA: We were having a laugh.

MARIE: Well, you take things too far Sam, you're a bit over the top sometimes.

SAMANTHA: Do you want to go in a minute?

MARIE: No.

V: Look Richard, why don't you come for Christmas dinner this year?

DON: So, you're back on him again now are you, we all like him again now?

V: You've been pestering me, Don, to give him a chance. I can't bloody win, me.

DON: No, let him come again. I tell you what Richard, come and they'll be a nice lovely surprise there for you from Santa, eh? I lovely shiny new bike, how's that?

RICHARD: I don't want a new bike, I want your bike.

V: How dare you say that to me!

DON: You what? He's not talking about you –

V: Oh Don, just ignore the twisted twat!

DON: Will you stop swearing Vanessa! I don't know why you're showing off all of a sudden. You're not impressing anyone.

V: Oh shut up Don, you've had a few now have you? Showing off? I'm speaking me mind.

RICHARD: Right, I think I'll call it a day.

V: Yes, go on Richard, leave your mess, go on – on your bike!

(Richard, Don and V start arguing. The following dialogue is heard above their noise by the audience.)

SAMANTHA: I tell you what Marie, I think your loving this.

MARIE: Don't push it Sam, or I really will say something.

SAMANTHA: Say something, I'm not bothered. Go on.

MARIE: I know you want me to.

GREG: She won't say owt.

SAMANTHA: I know she won't. Because she's a bully and she's really enjoying this, and that means more to her.

MARIE: Oh, I might, I'll see how I feel.

GREG: I'm like a little angel. I must be. I fly about on me own wings. But it can't come out, because then he has to know that he is lying, and if he's lying about that, maybe he's lying about the other things… in the past. And he has to let it go on really, because he owes them so much, both of them. I'm really pissed me, he's gonna throw me out in a minute. I know he's fucking watching me, waiting for me to go too far. I'll get thrown out and tomorrow I'll be on me wings again. Up there – whoosh! It's great. I can't help it. When you're grounded, you've got to do something to get by. I get out of it. I might throw a little bit of something in, just a taster.

(Next two lines are spoken at some point during Greg's speech.)

SAMANTHA: Don't.

MARIE: Why not?

SAMANTHA: I'm going. I don't even care Marie, I don't care what you say about me. Enjoy yourself.

(Samantha exits.)

V: Well, everyone's having a lovely night aren't they? That's why I love coming to pubs.

DON: Come on then, what are you doing?

RICHARD: I've got me bike.

DON: I'll ring you.

RICHARD: I'll come out with you.

V: I don't know why you're bothering.

DON: Oh, he'll think of a way to piss me off as we're getting in the car. Come on then, Richard.

MARIE: Bye Sir!

DON: Oh shut up. D'you know what you need to do love? Act your age!

(Don, Richard and V exit.)

(Marie looks around to find she might get stuck with Greg. She rolls her eyes and gets up to leave.)

MARIE: See you.

GREG: Yeah, ta-ra.

(Marie exits.)

Marie's enjoyed all that, she's had a good time. Sam didn't but she won't say owt, not ever now, not after she met V, no. It wasn't a chance meeting, Isobel had said they had the house to themselves tonight because his Mum was out for a meal and his Dad was meeting his brother here. Sam and Marie wanted to see, just to see what would happen, for different reasons. Because Sam is always thinking about it, and Marie wants to watch Sam. And it's still like that *(Does a lattice action with his hands.)* – it's not collapsed just yet. I'll have me wings on again tomorrow me. But when I'm grounded, I like these little things. He only lets me go so far, then I'm out. One time, she went to see Phil at Uni and she met his friend – younger, prettier Isobel, whose mum Marie used to pick on, because Mr Ashcroft looked after her, and no one gave a toss about Marie and her baby. Just one of the Radcliffes. No one'll say owt and it's that fucking delicate it's like this, it's like one of them like, sugar spun things you could fucking collapse it with a little bit of pressure. Sam never told a soul who the father was, no one, not even Isobel. Int life fucking complicated. And it's all so frail and they've all got a take on it. Journeys. I'm alright, I've got me wings. I'm gonna get one of them packets that have fourteen cigs in, they're only £3.10. It's not bad that is it? I don't know, I might be wrong. I might be surmising. I might be making it up, I don't know. I'm either pissed or flying aren't I? Me? There's no in-between. I can mither, but I'm not allowed to tinker. I know that much. But no one listens to me anyway, so he leaves it, 'til I get a bit telling, then I have to go. But as I always say, you don't know do you? I might be making it up, they're gone now. I've spoke to that Richard in here now and again, and I've seen both them birds in another boozer. I'm always listening in. Poor Richard, he's still a paperboy. He's done everything right and came out with nothing. I'm fucking wasted me. Where's me fucking halo? I'll need that tomorrow.

(Stands swaying for a bit and then goes out mumbling.)

Shit I think I left it on the bus. Oh it might be in the toilet I'll check on me way out. If some bastard's nicked it, etc...

THE
MAGI

Premiered at 53two, Manchester, 2018

The Magi is about the enduring love of a mother and daughter, who are poles apart in many ways.

It is a love letter to the close bond that can happen between a mother and child, and a celebration of neurodivergence and difference.

CAST (2)

SANDRA

Sandra is in her 70s, Sarah's mother, and is best taken with a pinch of salt. Anything she says that is harsh, uncomfortable or inconsiderate is measured, sharply thought-through and lands between a joke and self-effacing. She doesn't know why, but she also doesn't know why everyone else does it. She has all the traits of a personality disorder and autism but it manifests differently. Sandra cannot think about Sarah without her heart filling and growing twice the size. She is bold and open about her love for her daughter, immensely proud of her, and wonders at her talents.

SARAH

In her late 20s and Sandra's daughter. Sarah finds most situations that humans seem to think are interesting either excruciating or boring or both. She is intelligent and can write beautiful poetry at the drop of a hat, yet doesn't know why everyone else doesn't do it. Trying to mask her true self has cost her plenty. She's been vulnerable and in dark places which she didn't know how to navigate. She harbours anger towards Sandra for not being able to stop this, but also carries a core of molten love for her mother that never cools. When she was younger, her close relationship with her mum used to annoy her. After tonight, and every night thereafter, it will grow stronger.

SCENE 1

Before the lights come up, we hear the amazing intro played of Nina Simone's 'Little Girl Blue'.

Lights up, really bright, on a kitchen.

The dialogue is immediate and fast paced.

Sandra has a nice winter coat on that she is taking off, whilst Sarah is sat at a table in her dressing gown.

SANDRA: Why don't you move that flamin' mattress from the front garden?

SARAH: The council are coming for it.

SANDRA: You've got to keep on at them Sarah.

SARAH: I'm not as bothered about it as you are.

SANDRA: It's got stains on it.

SARAH: So?

SANDRA: It's awful, even you can see that.

SARAH: What's that supposed to mean? Even I can see that?

SANDRA: It means nothing, don't start reading into things.

SARAH: What do you mean 'even you can see that'?

SANDRA: Don't you care what people think of you?

SARAH: Not everyone. No.

(Pause.)

SANDRA: That's why you never get any Christmas cards from the neighbours.

SARAH: Oh well.

SANDRA: Just because you're mad you don't have to advertise it.

SARAH: Do you remember the family session Mum?

SANDRA: Phone them up tomorrow –

SARAH: When Dr Roberts said that word was inappropriate.

SANDRA: Just bloody phone them up.

SARAH: I'm not phoning them up tomorrow.

SANDRA: Don't then. Just leave it there.

SARAH: Tomorrow's Christmas Day.

(Pause.)

SANDRA: Well, tell them it's an emergency. They must have someone on call.

SARAH: Your embarrassment isn't an emergency.

SANDRA: Sarah, you've got a lovely wreath on the door and then a big piss-stained mattress against the hedges.

SARAH: For fuck's sake, I'll do it on Monday right?

SANDRA: Don't swear on Christmas Eve. Here. Merry Christmas.

(Sandra gives Sarah her present a hat and scarf, which Sarah takes and inspects.)

I've been knitting that scarf since September.

SARAH: Aww thanks Mum, that's lovely... I've made pasta, with the machine and a gorgonzola sauce.

SANDRA: Oh that sounds nice.

SARAH: I've done a pesto with pine nuts and a focaccia.

SANDRA: Oooooo lovely... I'm doing a goose tomorrow.

SARAH: Very Dickensian.

SANDRA: I won't be able to eat it all. Don't you get any meat for a week will you?

SARAH: I haven't got any meat since 2007.

SANDRA: You can have the rest, it'll see you right for ages.

SARAH: I don't eat it Mum.

SANDRA: Well, you can eat geese. Geese are bastards, Sarah. There's two near me always attacking people. Are we having wine?

SARAH: When we're eating, yes.

SANDRA: Why don't we just have one now?

SARAH: Because you'll start telling me when I went, as you say, mad. And then we'll have the Christmas row.

SANDRA: We've had the row. The mattress.

SARAH: That won't be it. And I'll end up drinking loads because you're here.

SANDRA: I knew it would be my fault. Is that what they told you in the bottom block?

SARAH: I'd prefer it if, when you talk about it to people, because I know you do, you use the hospital's name.

SANDRA: I do, I say the asylum. People are very surprised when I tell them how well-spoken the other inmates were.

SARAH: It wasn't a prison, Mum.

SANDRA: What did you talk about? With the rest of them?

SARAH: Things.

SANDRA: Like what? That woman opposite you was chatty.

SARAH: Fiona? She was a vet.

SANDRA: Oh. And now she's throwing shit at the wall.

SARAH: Is that supposed to be funny? We talked about what was wrong.

SANDRA: I could have told you that.

SARAH: Yeah. I talked about how you didn't hug me as a child.

SANDRA: I think it's time for wine.

SARAH: No, we're starting in on the row.

SANDRA: No, you're just picking on me.

SARAH: No, you're being horrible and I'm supposed to ignore it, and I'm not.

SANDRA: Okay... you never wanted a hug. Because you didn't like me.

SARAH: That's because you made me feel that I wasn't wanted.

SANDRA: You've made that up in your mind.

SARAH: You've got a short memory.

SANDRA: You've got all the answers, but there's one thing you haven't got?

SARAH: Don't do it Mum.

SANDRA: You know what you haven't got?

SARAH: It's not funny.

SANDRA: Your nose.

(Puts her thumb between her fingers to pretend she has Sarah's nose.)
(Pause.)

SARAH: Give it me.

SANDRA: I'll give it you when you stop picking on me.

(Sandra puts Sarah's 'nose' in her mouth, chews it, then pretends to spit-ball it out to Sarah, who catches it in the air and puts it back on.)

SARAH: I hate you.

SANDRA: You don't hate me, you know I did a good job with you.

SARAH: Yeah thanks, you were great.

SANDRA: Josie finds it very strange we don't spend the Christmas Day together you know?

SARAH: Tell her to get fucked.

SANDRA: No, I'm not going to tell her that am I, because she's giving me her old car, and you know that.

SARAH: Okay.

SANDRA: I told her I was coming seeing you today and she said 'Does she not come over on Christmas Day?' I'm doing her Salford accent. I said 'No, we like to spend Christmas Day on our own.' She went 'Oh. Right.' Like that. Then she said 'I'll be going to Rebecca's this year, last year it was Matthew's.'

SARAH: Rebecca's drawn the short straw this year then.

SANDRA: Yeah. Actually, Josie's been very stressed out.

SARAH: I thought your generation didn't get stressed, I thought you just got on with it.

SANDRA: Well, she's picked it up from somewhere along with the many invisible illnesses she has.

SARAH: I think we can do a wine now, do you want one Mum?

SANDRA: Yes, go on. Anyway, it's not good. You know her son, Matthew, has a sweet shop?

SARAH: Yes. I remember her telling me all the varieties. And then about his gated house in Alkrington and his heated car seats. Whilst I was when in hospital recovering from a breakdown.

SANDRA: To be fair Sarah, she was nervous that day, she thought that man wanted to strangle her.

SARAH: When in fact I did.

SANDRA: I brought her to shift focus from me. Like a shield.

SARAH: Right.

SANDRA: Anyway, she is so stressed-out Sarah, because Matthew's had to sell his business and sell his house and car because he was building up debts and no one knew. He has lost everything and gone bankrupt, right before Christmas.

(After a pause, Sarah laughs loudly and Sandra joins in.)

(Sandra 'cheers' Sarah and they take a big glug of wine.)

SARAH: I bet he was on the sherbert dabs.

SANDRA: Yes, they'll definitely be more to it, reading between the chocolate limes.

SARAH: Thanks Mum.

SANDRA: Thought you'd enjoy that. Where's my present by the way?

SARAH: I've done you a poem.

SANDRA: Oh. Is it made of chocolate?

SARAH: No.

SANDRA: I don't understand how it's a present then. Can I wear it?

SARAH: You will wear it, yes: I'll shove it up your arse.

(Sarah gets the card and throws it to Sandra who opens it.)

SANDRA:

I'm kidding, I'm kidding, read it me. I'll close me eyes. *(Closes eyes.)*

SARAH: *(Reads.)*

'The matriarchal sparkle
Blinds the child to the debacle
At the table, topped with hot dry goods
Though the paper-hatted girl adores
The box the expensive toy came in
Love from her mother
Was the greatest prize

Imagine that famous journey
To surprise a child and see a mum's delight?
Who would not follow any starry night
To lift the spirits of a family in exodus
With scents and sweets and tell them
They are here to save the world?
Any family
Anywhere
Is the light shining saving grace
Of this hopeful helpless human race
Any person
Anywhere
Is happiest whenever they see the kindness
In one another's face

I would gladly make the trek
With the magi
Just to see the twinkle
In that mother's eye'

SANDRA: *(Opens eyes.)* You wouldn't though would you, because you don't believe in God. That was last year's Christmas row. *(Swigs the wine.)*

SARAH: I remember.

SANDRA: You know when I think you started to go ill?

SARAH: When?

SANDRA: When you had shingles. Why you looking at me like that? I said ill, I didn't say mad.

SARAH: I might get a cat you know, something to love.

SANDRA: Oh don't Sarah, you won't take care of it.

SARAH: I'm going for a fag in the back.

(Exits.)

SANDRA: *(Shouts towards the back.)* It'll shit all over.

(During the following action the same song from the beginning picks up from when it left off.)

(Sarah comes back in for the new scarf. Sandra, assuming Sarah has left the room, picks up the card, holds it close to her heart and gently wells up with love. Sarah watches this unseen, pulls the scarf up to her nose, smells it, then wraps it around herself like a hug.)

(As the lights go down we see a smile on both their faces.)

This play confronts the clash and competition of middle-class age and working-class youth, fear, love, loss and bereavement. All played out within a Mancunian tower block in the mid-noughties.

CAST (4)

BRIDGETTE

Aged around 60, well-spoken, engagingly flowery, but sometimes cruel.

RONNIE

A man of around 60, patient, logical and very dry, married to Bridgette.

OTIS

A fiery, scary, but loving man in his 30s, married to Paula.

PAULA

In her 30s, matriarchal and confident.

ACT ONE, SCENE 1

Bridgette is rummaging in a box. She is dressed in an odd mismatch of casual and formal wear with a padded farm coat on over the top.

We hear the toilet flush and Ronnie enters. He has a short-sleeved check shirt on, khaki slacks and white trainers. He has the same type of coat on as Bridgette.

BRIDGETTE: Do you let gravity dictate everything Ronnie? Let the crap control you? Are you that scared of the consequences that you've now become terrified of a little bit of pain? A small amount of discomfort and you choose to avoid it by letting things just fall out of you? Do you just sit there and allow the shit to just seep out at leisure? You just wait like a fool there for as long as it takes for the shite to plop down. I mean, are you that much of a weed now, that you can't even thrutch a little bit?

RONNIE: I didn't realise you were waiting for the bathroom.

BRIDGETTE: I'm not. Probably just as well, since you've been in there relishing in it for an hour. That's the difference between me and you, I force change, I'm not scared. I've given birth.

RONNIE: Now, you see, you think you can do something and you wind up getting in a mess with it and needing help.

BRIDGETTE: I think there's something missing, it's a lead or something.

(Ronnie quickly assembles the CD player.)

RONNIE: I'm not taking over, or assuming you don't know how to assemble it, I just think I may have some useful input.

BRIDGETTE: And?

RONNIE: There's something missing.

BRIDGETTE: Oh so I'm right?

RONNIE: No. I just wanted you to experience a moment of triumph, it's all here. Find a hole for the thing…

BRIDGETTE: I still feel the same, all slumpy. Sludgy. I feel like a slug Ronnie.

RONNIE: Let's have something nice on.

BRIDGETTE: Yes. Let's listen to something nice. Put a bit of sugar on the shit.

RONNIE: Don't be stupid.

(Bridgette finds this very amusing.)

> **BRIDGETTE:** It's like a little hutch Ronnie. Like a hutch. Rabbits don't live long you know?
>
> **RONNIE:** Don't they?
>
> **BRIDGETTE:** No.
>
> **RONNIE:** Where's the bag with the CDs in it?
>
> **BRIDGETTE:** Have-a-look-for-it.
>
> **RONNIE:** I see.
>
> **BRIDGETTE:** We didn't think clearly enough about this.
>
> **RONNIE:** There isn't the time.
>
> **BRIDGETTE:** You don't start all set up for life. It's not going to make any difference.
>
> **RONNIE:** It was your decision. Shut up about it now.
>
> **BRIDGETTE:** Don't tell me to shut up.
>
> **RONNIE:** Shut up Bridgette.
>
> **BRIDGETTE:** Don't say it again.
>
> **RONNIE:** Shut up.

(There is a slight pause, then Bridgette rummages in a box, finds a shoe, throws it at Ronnie and hits him on the nose.)

> **BRIDGETTE:** Don't speak to me like that again and don't feel sorry for yourself, idiot!

(Ronnie runs into the bathroom, then comes out with a tissue to his nose and his head held up.)

(His anger boils over and he picks up a box, launches one object after the other at Bridgette, then eventually the cardboard box. She manages to escape unscathed and begins to put the objects back into the box.)

> **RONNIE:** Don't pack them away again, put them away now.
>
> **BRIDGETTE:** When we started, we said didn't we – 'We're making a go of it.' You know, going together and making a go of it. What's this called then Ronnie?
>
> **RONNIE:** It's called considering the future.
>
> **BRIDGETTE:** But... well, why don't we just live separately then?
>
> **RONNIE:** Because we can't afford to and we love each other.
>
> **BRIDGETTE:** Oh we do, yes, I forgot. I thought it was just familiarity and erm... what's that thing animals do? But it's love is it? You know... I love this vase more than you?

RONNIE: I know you do darling.

BRIDGETTE: I love an object more than you. The object of my affection.

RONNIE: Yes Bridgette, and no doubt it will outlive me.

BRIDGETTE: Even if it doesn't, I'll miss it more than I'll miss you when you die Ronnie.

(Bridgette sets off laughing, looking at Ronnie and the vase.)

It's not funny, it's true.

RONNIE: There's a couple down below us with a child.

BRIDGETTE: I've heard it.

RONNIE: I wonder if it's going to be a problem.

BRIDGETTE: I imagine so. Probably grow up to take over the home it grew up in and turn it into some Habi-twatted nightmare.

RONNIE: I meant if it would be pestering, talking to us.

BRIDGETTE: Do you know she immediately ripped out the wood around the sink? What for?

RONNIE: She didn't, he did.

BRIDGETTE: Yes he did. Probably pissed all over the house now like a dog leaving its scent.

RONNIE: Why would he want to do that?

BRIDGETTE: I'm being clever, why would he do that? Idiot!

RONNIE: Bridgette, it's too late for all this now. Can you go and get some stamps from the shop?

BRIDGETTE: No I can't. Can't you? What do we need stamps for? We've not moved to another country Ronnie.

RONNIE: There's letters need addressing.

BRIDGETTE: The place is just about things now. Bric-a-brac they have.

RONNIE: She's making it her own. You did that, it's her turn now.

BRIDGETTE: No I didn't idiot. I perused carefully. I didn't plough through a shopping centre and slaver over fixtures and fittings. I took years to get what we have.

RONNIE: Well, it's much more convenient now my love, where do you want the fruit bowl?

BRIDGETTE: I want it in the window. I want people to see we're healthy.

RONNIE: So shall I put the wooden apples back in it, or are we going to buy real fruit and let it rot in front of our eyes again?

BRIDGETTE: Fuck off. Get the fridge ready. Fridges are a danger, with moving.

(Pause.)

I'm not going to be able to cope with this. This isn't acceptable; I can't see us being able to live here.

RONNIE: Bridgette, I will only say this once – I won't let you make this difficult for her –

BRIDGETTE: What?

RONNIE: Even if it's because you don't realise you're doing so. I will not let you make this difficult for her.

BRIDGETTE: If you had a brain, I would think that you were saying that to stab me in the heart. But since you don't and have no idea how life actually works, because you're an idiot, I can ignore you.

RONNIE: I won't let you make this difficult for her!

BRIDGETTE: After saying you would only say it once you've said it about five times you fool! If you want to make a serious point, think it through properly.

RONNIE: You will NOT MAKE THIS DIFFICULT FOR HER BRIDGETTE!

BRIDGETTE: And here it comes again!

(Ronnie runs at Bridgette and covers her mouth.)

RONNIE: Give yourself five minutes okay? Stop or I will strangle you. I don't want to do that. Because we have to do this, so please, in the nicest possible way and because I love you, just shut up!

(They both begin to cry and hold each other, then laugh and cry again.)

(Knock at the door.)

BRIDGETTE: Go on.

RONNIE: No, I can't answer the door like this.

BRIDGETTE: It's okay, it might be the sofa. Go on. I've done now. Come here.

(Wipes his eyes and kisses him.)

(Ronnie exits and enters with Otis and Paula.)

RONNIE: Bridgette, this is er...

OTIS: Hiya, I'm Otis and this is my life partner Paula. We've got a key for you. Tina asked us to give you these, she forgot. They're for the bathroom window. Yeah, it's dead easy, ours is the same, you're best off locking them, I know it's high up, but you can't take chances can you?

PAULA: Was you from a farm?

RONNIE: No.

OTIS: What's with the coats then?

PAULA: We thought you must've moved from a farm.

BRIDGETTE: No, we have a house in Delph.

RONNIE: We had a house in Delph, our daughter lives there now. And we're living here.

BRIDGETTE: We don't live anywhere yet!

(Pause, too long and weird.)

OTIS: The bloke at the bottom used to live in San Francisco.

(Pause.)

I think he's a puff –

PAULA: Otis!

OTIS: Where's your telly going? Ours is over here. Just got a new one, brilliant sound. An horse can set off, and it sounds like it goes from our kitchen through the bedroom, right the way through till it's behind us. Outstanding it is.

BRIDGETTE: Thank you for the key.

RONNIE: I hear you have a baby?

OTIS: No, she's not a baby.

BRIDGETTE: Oh, we thought we heard crying earlier.

PAULA: No, she wouldn't have been crying.

OTIS: Yeah, that's our Charlotte...

PAULA: She's weren't crying, she doesn't cry a lot. She's just loud and confident.

OTIS: She's got a gob on her, but she's a good girl.

PAULA: Yeah, she's dead good. Otis has the telly too loud so she has to shout over it.

BRIDGETTE: Well, she's very quite now.

OTIS: That's 'cause she's gone to Failsworth.

BRIDGETTE: Oh.

OTIS: We're gonna get pissed in a bit and have a lie in tomorrow.

BRIDGETTE: Thank you for the key.

PAULA: You're welcome.

(Pause.)

RONNIE: Yes, thank you.

PAULA: Right, come on.

OTIS: Alright, come on. Welcome in anyway. Welcome in to the building.

(They go to exit, then Otis returns.)

If you want anything, we're just below you. It's nice here, might not be as nice as Delph but me and Paula are alright. Sorry, see you later. Sorry.

(Otis exits.)

RONNIE: It is quite nice here.

BRIDGETTE: Ronnie, why do you make the most of everything?

RONNIE: Because, there isn't the time for anything else.

BRIDGETTE: She should have wanted me to stay there.

RONNIE: Yes, but she didn't and quite frankly neither would you and she's being like you.

BRIDGETTE: I hate that couple.

RONNIE: Why don't you invite them up later, you'd enjoy picking on them. I could do with the break.

BRIDGETTE: Yes, I would enjoy that. I will do that if it's okay with you. I'll go down there later and be charming and invite them up. Put a bit of sugar on the shit.

(This following dialogue is heartbreaking for Bridgette.)

I don't want to live here. I don't want it to happen and I know it won't change anything but I have to say it isn't fair.

RONNIE: No it isn't fair. I'm going to make us a sandwich now before the couch comes. Then I'm going to phone Emily and we'll tell her how much we love the flat.

BRIDGETTE: And don't say I didn't like what they did with the wood around the sink. And tell her the neighbours are lovely. And ask if she's okay, but don't tell her I asked, just ask in your way.

ACT ONE, SCENE 2

Lights up on the flat, now with a sofa and two chairs.

Otis and Paula sit on the sofa and Ronnie and Bridgette on the chairs. Otis and Ronnie have a can each, Bridgette and Paula have a glass of wine.

During the first section of dialogue, Bridgette exits and re-enters with a glass for both Ronnie and Otis. She stares at the cans until Ronnie pours his into the glass. Otis attempts to follow suit, but Paula pours it back into his can and uses the glass as an ashtray.

OTIS: ...So, he comes back from the bog, the dog's only sat on Duggie's stool! He goes fucking mad! That's what it's like you see, regulars and that. They don't like anything different happening.

RONNIE: And do you enjoy working in a bar, Otis?

OTIS: I do yeah, I love it. I'd love me own pub. There wasn't a manager's job before I worked there you know? They created that for me.

BRIDGETTE: And do you have a lot of staff?

PAULA: There's only him works there in the day –

OTIS: Yes but I have duties, I do the time sheets –

PAULA: Who for?

OTIS: Alright Paul, don't take the piss!

PAULA: They don't give a shit what job you do!

OTIS: I'm just explaining alright? They asked me didn't they?

PAULA: He does enjoy it, it suits him, he'd love a pub, but I don't think it would be nice for Charlotte, all that smoke and pissed-up people.

OTIS: She wouldn't have to see any of it, she'd be upstairs!

PAULA: What, stuck upstairs all the time like a prisoner, no garden?

OTIS: There's no fucking garden now.

(Pause.)

PAULA: There's me Mum's garden.

OTIS: So, would your Mum not have a garden, if we had a pub?

PAULA: I'm not moving into a pub!

OTIS: Right! We'll just live here forever then!

PAULA: Or you get a pub and I'll live here! Just ignore us.

BRIDGETTE: Yes. Do you work at the bar, Paula?

PAULA: No, I work at Manchester Museum. Looking after the artefacts.

OTIS: Do you fuck!

PAULA: Otis, I play an important role at the Museum.

OTIS: Yeah but you're hardly dusting down fossils with a blusher brush are you Paul?

PAULA: Who polishes Asru the Temple Chantress's head? Who gets rid of all fingerprints and dirty marks off the cabinets? And I do that on top of manning reception. There's nothing I don't know about Egyptology.

RONNIE: Well, that's surprisingly interesting isn't it my love? We didn't expect that did we?

BRIDGETTE: And who looks after little Charlotte when you're at work?

PAULA: She goes to a day nursery.

BRIDGETTE: I really feel for mums now, it's such a shame they have to work and miss out on the childhood of their little ones.

PAULA: Well, I only work Monday to Friday.

BRIDGETTE: I was quite lucky really; I got to spend every day with my daughter until she went to school. And is she okay when you leave her, she doesn't cry for you?

PAULA: No, she loves it.

RONNIE: Otis. That's an unusual name?

BRIDGETTE: Well, yes I'm sure. My Emily broke her heart when she started school, because she was so used to spending all her time with her Mum you see she didn't want to leave me though she did grow to school eventually, loved to learn –

PAULA: Oh, I hated school me –

OTIS: Me Mam liked Otis Reading.

RONNIE: I see. And do you?

BRIDGETTE: I taught her to read you see, gave her a good head start.

OTIS: He's alright; he can carry a tune, not as good as me like.

RONNIE: Ha ha, yes. Is Charlotte named after a singer?

PAULA: I use to pretend I'd read the books we had at school –

BRIDGETTE: It's important to read to your children –

PAULA: I know, I always read Charlotte a bedtime story –

OTIS: No, she's named after a spider.

RONNIE: Oh, ha ha yes, Charlotte's Web, yes, I remember reading that to Emily, ha ha.

OTIS: She was very kind and wise wasn't she? Charlotte the spider?

BRIDGETTE: I hope they're reading to her in day care. I expect they don't get chance to have a one-to-one with the children –

PAULA: They're dead good with them –

BRIDGETTE: Oh, I'm sure. I'm sure most of them love children, that's why they do it isn't it? Yes, I'm sure they're very careful these days after those incidents, you know. When they had a revealing hidden camera and the helpers were smacking the children when they were crying? But like you say, Charlotte doesn't cry for you so...

PAULA: Yeah, well, I know quite a few of them that work there and they're very nice. It's a lovely place isn't it, Otis?

OTIS: Oh yeah, she loves it, always coming back with pasta drawings and that.

PAULA: It is hard leaving her, but at the end of the day, I think to myself, well, at least I get to get her nice things and have a lovely holiday with her.

BRIDGETTE: Of course, of course, like I say, I was very lucky that Ronnie could support us on the one wage.

PAULA: Oh, I think I'd still work me, I like me freedom, wouldn't want to be stuck at home all day.

BRIDGETTE: I used to take Emily to parks a lot.

PAULA: What even in the rain?

BRIDGETTE: No, not in the rain.

PAULA: 'Cause dunt it rain a lot in Oldham?

BRIDGETTE: We didn't live in Oldham.

PAULA: Well, you know, on the hills? It's freezing int it?

BRIDGETTE: It's a beautiful place for a child to grow up.

PAULA: I bet it is, yeah. Just a bit cold though.

BRIDGETTE: Beautiful, lovely scenery, not that we had to go very far anyway, we had a lovely big garden.

PAULA: There's a park across the road you know? Very well looked after. That's the best thing about parks, it's all done for you, I can't be doing with gardening.

RONNIE: Yes, and there was a prize pig wasn't there?

OTIS: She dies in the end dunt she? I might not read it to Char; I don't want her to be sad. I won't buy Bambi me, no, she won't be watching that. I think the world of her, me.

RONNIE: Yes.

(Lights down.)

(Lights up.)

(It's later in the evening, everyone is quite drunk. Some music is on and everyone except Bridgette has changed places.)

OTIS: I'm dead happy me. There is a heaven Ronnie, and it's just below you.

RONNIE: Really, well, that's handy. I imagined hell would be the one below.

OTIS: I never thought I could love a girl as much as Paula but Paul's just had to face facts. What's your little princess called? Emma?

RONNIE: Emily, not little anymore though –

OTIS: I bet she is in your eyes Ronnie.

RONNIE: Yes.

OTIS: So she lives in your house then?

RONNIE: Yes.

OTIS: You sold it to her?

RONNIE: No, we finished paying our mortgage and her husband had bought this flat to rent out and she wanted to live back at home so we gave her the house.

OTIS: Fucking hell! Now there's a daddy's girl for you!

RONNIE: Oh yes.

OTIS: Fucking hell, did you hear that Paul?

PAULA: They gave their house to their daughter?

BRIDGETTE: Actually, her husband David bought us a flat –

PAULA: He bought you a flat round here and moved into your house!

OTIS: Eh, I said to him, that's a daddy's girl!

PAULA: Too right! I don't even think you'd be that daft would you?

OTIS: Er, I wouldn't be having any fucking bloke marrying my daughter and turfing me out.

PAULA: It could happen though babe.

BRIDGETTE: Let's have a toast shall we? Let's toast Paula and Otis and little Charlotte, I hope she has everything Emily has had, I mean that – cheers!

RONNIE: Yes, we wish your little girl all from life our daughters had –

BRIDGETTE: We certainly do, everything!

OTIS: Int that lovely Paul?

PAULA: Yes.

(Silently mouths 'weirdoes' to Otis.)

RONNIE: Cheers to the young man with the famous name, his wife with the man's name, and his daughter with a spider's name, cheers!

BRIDGETTE: Cheers! Here's to heaven below us!

OTIS: Let's toast the mad couple who took cupboard love to the extent they gave her the fucking house! Awkward.

PAULA: Awww, you'll have it nice though, with your stuff.

(Bridgette rummages through a box and finds a photo of Emily.)

BRIDGETTE: This is a picture of my daughter when she graduated from university.

(Hands the photo to Paula.)

PAULA: Awww, she's very pretty.

BRIDGETTE: She is very much like Ronnie and his side of the family.

PAULA: Yeah, she's got his eyes, and his big hands. But it's someone else. He'are, Otis'll know –

(Otis looks at the photo.)

OTIS: Alien.

PAULA: That's her. Alien. What's her name now? Aliens, what's her name now –

OTIS: Ghostbusters.

PAULA: What's her name...?

OTIS: Thelma and Louise –

PAULA: No not her –

RONNIE: Sigourney Weaver?

PAULA: Yeah! She looks like her. Very beautiful, she looks tall, you can tell by her hands and her neck. Very prominent cheek bones.

RONNIE: Yes, she is very beautiful.

PAULA: She's very serious.

OTIS: Yeah, big cheekbones, like a bit of a man's face, but a pretty man.

PAULA: I thought she would be. I'd hate to be famous though me, I bet your ears are burning all the time.

(Pause.)

(Otis looks at Paula and then laughs as if it has been catapulted out of his throat into the room.)

OTIS: That's classic that –

PAULA: What, they would be –

OTIS: Oh wait 'til I tell 'em at work. Ears burning. You're funny you –

PAULA: Well, they would. Left for love, right for spite. All the time. Where's that picture of Charlotte?

OTIS: Oh it's not that good, go and get the album.

PAULA: No, I can't be arsed, get that one out.

(Otis takes a photo from his wallet and hands it to Ronnie.)

OTIS: He'are. It was ages ago though this, her hair went a lot thicker –

PAULA: And them chubby cheeks went.

RONNIE: She has very beautiful eyes.

PAULA: I know. They're lovely aren't they?

OTIS: That's in this park here that. It looks sunny but it was a freezing autumn morning. A Saturday morning it was. Paula loved this coat.

PAULA: I loved that coat! I always said that if I ever have a girl I'm gonna get her a red coat like Red Riding Hood, so I saw this coat in –

BRIDGETTE: Isn't it funny, do you remember that Ronnie? When a coat was exciting? Oh it's been years since we thought about silly things like that isn't it, Ronnie? Isn't it sad? I bet she's grown out of the coat now. Oh, I do hope you have more memories than the coat. It would be such a shame not to remember her childhood. Mind, I expect she's spending most of her weekends in Failsworth.

RONNIE: It's been a long day for us, it's all change. We're feeling a bit out of the ordinary.

(Bridgette begins to neck a bottle of spirits.)

PAULA: I'm thinking now, it was in Next I think, I thought, I'm gonna get that, and it'll fit one day.

BRIDGETTE: Failsworth, now there's a shithole! No, no, I can say that you see, I was brought up there. I bet I know your Mum.

PAULA: I don't think so.

BRIDGETTE: The scruff pots we were, she'll remember me. I was the youngest of the Walkers. I wore my sister's old shoes until I was sixteen. Sixteen when I got a job tying up fat old ladies' corsets in Washington's Credit Drapers on Queen Street. I spent my luncheon vouchers dancing in the Ritz. I didn't dare tell me Dad. Not that he would know anyway... pissed-up and pissed off. I got an escape route you see, I could sing and dance and I hot-footed out of there the minute I got the chance.

PAULA: Me Mum loves it in Failsworth, she lives right near Daisy Nook.

BRIDGETTE: The pig farm!

OTIS: I love Failsworth baths me. You know, next to the school? I take Char sometimes after we've picked her up.

BRIDGETTE: I used to go to Broadway baths, the only chance we ever got to have a decent wash! Old Victorian baths, probably the fucking same still.

RONNIE: Stop swearing Bridgette, it doesn't suit you.

BRIDGETTE: I am an excellent swimmer you know?

RONNIE: Yes you are, the best swimmer I've ever known.

BRIDGETTE: I can glide through the water; it's like flying to me. I am magnificent.

RONNIE: Swimming is such a useful skill isn't it?

BRIDGETTE: Swimming is the most important skill a child can learn. Forget tying shoelaces, they're practically obsolete. Forget riding a bike, who needs to know how to ride a bike in a crisis?

OTIS: No, it's always good to know how to ride a bike.

BRIDGETTE: But it won't save your life will it?

OTIS: It might do –

BRIDGETTE: How could knowing how to ride a bike save a person's life?

OTIS: Well, either you could be in a crisis situation and your car has broken down, but because you're going on a bike riding holiday you have your bike on the roof rack and can ride of in the middle of nowhere to get help.

PAULA: Or, you could be out riding on it, someone attacks you and you can throw it at them?

OTIS: Or you're on safari on bikes, and a lion is coming towards you, not a cheetah though, they'd be quicker than a bike.

PAULA: Don't be stupid. I bet a lion could still outrun you. You wouldn't be used to Africa. Anyway, there wouldn't be a safari bike ride, it's too dangerous.

RONNIE: Knowing how to swim is a very important skill. I'm not very good at swimming.

BRIDGETTE: Ronnie's a terrible swimmer, he's too solid.

RONNIE: Bridgette is a wonderful swimmer. She glides through the water.

BRIDGETTE: I could swim for miles; it's no effort for me.

RONNIE: I flay around in the hope I'll stay afloat.

BRIDGETTE: I glide without effort.

RONNIE: It's a skill.

BRIDGETTE: It's a skill, a way of thinking about the water. You couldn't do it, you've no idea. You don't know the first thing about swimming. She should've seen that.

RONNIE: It's not important now.

BRIDGETTE: You don't feel safe when someone teaches you how to ride a fucking bike, liberated maybe. Maybe too independent, too assured you can take off, but when someone teaches you how to swim, you love them for that. Half of the world is terrifying to you, if you can't swim. You can get by without shoelaces or a fucking bike. It's a closeness you see, it's a physical closeness, trusting that person not to let go too soon, but I would have never let go. I should've been the one to teach her to swim. But she didn't know I was capable of that, because you were so shit at it, she thought I would be worse. The one thing I could do better than you. So she's terrified of the water like you. I think she would've looked at me differently if I could have taught her that. But she just used to scream and shiver in my arms. She just couldn't trust me to get something right. And it's too late now, she'll never know how good I am, and it's all because you don't like the water. I should've done that, but you ruined that for me. And that's why Ronnie, we made a mistake. We should've trusted me more. You with your stupid philosophies and phrases.

PAULA: I taught Char to swim.

BRIDGETTE: Oh who gives a shit!

PAULA: There's a baths down the road you know? I take her all the time.

BRIDGETTE: Oh is there? Well isn't that lovely?!

PAULA: You're not the only family in the world you know.

OTIS: I tell you what Ronnie, heaven is below you. And it's the best thing that's ever happened to me.

BRIDGETTE: This is absolute horror.

PAULA: We're happy, we have everything we need.

OTIS: Heaven's below you Bridgette, you should know that.

BRIDGETTE: Well at least I don't have to go that far then, for heaven.

RONNIE: I think it's time to wrap it up now.

OTIS: I've got me wife, had me kid, that's enough.

BRIDGETTE: That's not enough.

PAULA: We've got everything us, starting out, making a go of it.

OTIS: We don't know what will happen, but we just hope for the best. Do our best, build our life up.

RONNIE: Yes, build up your life, see what happens. That's all you can do.

BRIDGETTE: It ends in remorse, regret, and an abundance of self-hatred.

RONNIE: No Bridgette, that's not fair, I have a lifetime of fond memories.

BRIDGETTE: Ronnie, you look older now.

RONNIE: You don't Bridgette, you look like a child. A little girl who's lost her dolly.

OTIS: Hmmm, think we better call it a night then.

BRIDGETTE: You're only going to make the same mistakes as we did.

PAULA: No way. I would never choose that furniture for our flat.

BRIDGETTE: My daughter never truly loved me.

PAULA: I wouldn't have that kind of furniture.

BRIDGETTE: My daughter...

PAULA: I do the best I can. I think that will be right or this will be right, I don't know. You never know whether you're happy and getting on with it. Or... what's the other one...?

OTIS: Stop talking now; you're doing everyone's head in.

PAULA: It's not me, I was alright. It's them two pecking.

RONNIE: Otis, I have a lovely malt, would you like to have a dram with me?

OTIS: Yes, Ronnie, I would.

PAULA: Bridgette, would you like a Bacardi Breezer?

BRIDGETTE: No.

PAULA: Well, fuck off then! Come on babe, let's go.

OTIS: Paul, I love you to bits, but I'm having a drink with Ronnie, you can go and leave us to it. I'll come down with you, there's something I want to show Ronnie.

PAULA: I will, I am.

BRIDGETTE: It's late Ronnie –

RONNIE: Go to bed, Bridgette.

(The women exit.)

(Ronnie goes to the kitchen, Otis goes downstairs, and in a minute they both return. Ronnie has whisky and a glass, Otis has a teddy.)

OTIS: D'you know what to do with this Ronnie, it's been driving me mad all day? See, she loves this teddy, but no matter how much I turn the legs and arms, it's still not right.

RONNIE: Let me have a look...

(Ronnie turns the legs and arms for a while, it still doesn't look right. He's getting frustrated; Otis retrieves it and gently turns the head the right way.)

OTIS: How annoying is that?

RONNIE: Bridgette is very, very upset. You can't imagine how this is.

OTIS: I know, I sort of guessed, with the swimming shit. Your daughter's ill int she? If it was Charl, me life would end.

RONNIE: It's a process, I can't do that yet.

OTIS: No way am I saying do yourself in. I'm just saying I would feel like that. How do you manage? How do you carry on?

RONNIE: It's a process, Bridgette needs me, Emily needs us, you can't be selfish. We spent our whole lives building up our home; our daughter had the best we could offer. The seams were loose, the genes were wrong. We did our best.

OTIS: Okay. But I think your wife is mixed-up about how she deals with it...

RONNIE: She wouldn't say anything to upset Emily.

OTIS: No. I know. Paula takes offence at someone, she never says owt to them, she just makes my life a misery with it. Then if I say or do summat that annoys her, she simmers over it for a week and then attacks me out of the blue. Like the other week I was meant to be home at tea, but I stayed out in the bar after work, phoned her and that. She goes 'fine' which I fall for every time. Never heard any complaint about it, then four days later came home from work, on time by the way, walked into the kitchen, she threw a can opener at me head! Then it all comes out then – 'I had made you chilli. I had the candles lit, Charlotte was at me Mum's.' You don't know what you gonna get when you walk in, it's exciting.

RONNIE: I'd rather take the flack. I just don't want her making this difficult for Emily. Emily is going to live in the house until... she... they had only been able to rent a council flat, and then, once they had enough for a mortgage they could only afford to buy in this flat's price range. Then we discovered she was very ill... It didn't seem right to buy a place and so... Bridgette asked her what she wanted to do, she said she wished she could live in the home she grew up in, as if she had owned it and built it up herself, time was short and that's what she wanted. So without really thinking it through, Bridgette felt that she had really done something that Emily wished for.

OTIS: Now you're here.

RONNIE: We asked David to buy a flat so that David could have somewhere to live after. When a situation like that happens you don't think clearly, you want to do what the person wants and not what seems, in the bigger sense, the right thing.

OTIS: You couldn't have really said no, could you? Must be some house that.

RONNIE: It's a lovely home. It's kept us together, and now... well, I don't know.

OTIS: You think a lot of her though don't you... you're keen on Bridgette?

RONNIE: Oh, I am keen on her, I love her, of course I do, yes. I want to kill her but, well, we're very close and I imagine that to be normal, to be honest. Bridgette, when I met her, she was a student teacher at the school I taught at. She was a musical theatre actress from being very young and she was quite a liberated woman. She didn't really want to be a teacher. Once we married and had Emily, she devoted herself to Emily and the house and then Emily went to school and Bridgette just had the house, she went back to work eventually, but she loved the house.

OTIS: Paula works at the Museum, you know?

RONNIE: Yes, she said.

OTIS: She knows all about the collections. She feels like she looks after them. She don't, but she thinks she does.

RONNIE: Yes, she said.

OTIS: She told me about this thing, it's the Egyptian thing. They have this section, it's called The Beautiful House, and in there, that's where they take all the brains and insides out of the dead. It's meant to be the most sacred place. That's why they call it The Beautiful House, the most precious parts of a person get put into jars they can take onto the next world.

RONNIE: More baggage!

OTIS: I know! They build these things, so they can preserve themselves, and what for? More baggage! Are you having that Ronnie?

RONNIE: You would think wouldn't you, that death was the ultimate. What purpose would that serve?

OTIS: I know! When I go, you can throw me on a skip and have done with it.

RONNIE: But how would that be, for your family? It would be like you didn't deserve respect.

OTIS: But when I'm gone, I'm gone, what's left?

RONNIE: Everything's left. Your memories. Everything's left in things, things that belonged to them...

(Makes a noise as if to black that thought out.)

Anyway, you're very upbeat aren't you Otis? It's good to know that it isn't all shit – the world!

OTIS: Oh I'm optimistic. We're good people, we do no harm, we want a nice life, why not? Anyway, you'll see, it's a nice place to live, you're just used to something bigger. Cheers.

ACT ONE, SCENE 3

Otis and Paula's.

Bridgette has come round to apologise. She sits uncomfortably opposite Paula, who is feeling just as uncomfortable.

PAULA: See what I mean about the telly? You can hear it wherever you're sat, don't know why he has it so loud. I've got a lot of Egyptian souvenirs from the Museum, you'll notice. They're me favourite, in the gift shop. Not just the gift shop, I mean, the collections. They're me favourite.

BRIDGETTE: Yes. They're very nice. Very... gold.

PAULA: Not on purpose! I'm not really ostentatious; it's just that a lot of the things are gold. They're like, prizes, I suppose. Prizes of their lives, what they deserved or... gathered... by being... high up.

BRIDGETTE: I've come to apologise about –

PAULA: It's okay, I don't get easily offended. I can put things to the back of me mind you see. Otis can't, his mind doesn't have a back. It's just there, all the time, shooting out from his mouth. That's what I like about him. The man's incapable of letting things fester, he's rubbish at lying. Otis said you used to be in musicals.

BRIDGETTE: Oh a long time ago.

PAULA: Any big ones?

BRIDGETTE: Well, some well-known yes, at the time. I was in the original cast of Hair.

PAULA: Don't know that one. What about Starlight Express – I can see you in pair of roller boots.

BRIDGETTE: No. My days were over long before that came along.

PAULA: Cats?

BRIDGETTE: No.

PAULA: Oh. Don't know any others before Cats. Is that where you met Ronnie?

BRIDGETTE: No. I met Ronnie when I started teaching English, Ronnie taught Chemistry.

PAULA: Yeah, I can see that. He's got that boring tone. Don't tell him.

BRIDGETTE: He knows, I've told him. Many times. You have done a lot with the flat.

PAULA: Yeah, I have. It wasn't anything like this when we first moved in. It's totally different now. The floors had, erm… floor tiles; I got rid of them straight away. Then whilst there was no floor down I scraped the walls. 'Bout twenty years of wallpaper, underneath woodchip by the way. Took me a week. That's just in this room. There was aertex in the kitchen and the bathroom, woodchip in both bedrooms. Anyway, once that was done, we had to have it plastered; half of it came off with the paper, cracks all over the place. So Otis's brother Ray plastered it all. And there, at the side of all the windows, they'd done a really bad job of it. What it was, was the council put in new windows a year before we moved in and there was massive gaps. I put caulking in, after Ray had plastered, then I sanded it down. So it was like a blank canvas…

(Bridgette thinks Paula has finished.)

…then I thought, I'm not having carpets, but we couldn't just put flooring down because the floor was uneven… it would've cracked you see? So Ray and Otis put this levelling stuff down, right the way through. We had to leave a good few days before we could even stand on it. Might have been a week. No, it wasn't that long. Maybe it was. You'd have to ask Otis. So anyway, after that, we had flooring put in everywhere but the bathroom and toilet. Otis just wanted to get lino for in there but I said no, we'll tile it, the walls were half tiled and I said we'll just match it up; it's much easier to clean. So I tiled it myself, got myself an angle grinder and grout and a book from the library and did it. I thought blue mosaic for the bathroom, so I saw this style, I thought hard to cut because they were a funny shape, like pebbles, like, bobbly round the sides, but it turned out, they were easier, because they were sort of easier to put down and you couldn't really tell if there was any mistakes. But they didn't really match up with the square tiles halfway up the walls. But luckily, I saw these transfers with, like pebbles on, they're not an exact match but they're not far off. The ones on the floor are a bit of a deeper blue; the ones on the wall are slightly lighter and a tiny bit green. But once we put them lights in, you can't tell, it's only in the daytime you can tell, and it's only us use it then usually so I don't really mind. I just got black and white tiles for the toilet, then got some tile paint and painted every other square up the wall black. And in both rooms I painted the walls white. I think that's best for a bathroom. The kitchen, I went for Mexican. Multicoloured wall tiles, plates, chilli pepper fairy lights and yellow walls and orange laminate on all the cupboards. We weren't gonna have a breakfast bar but Otis got a couple of spare stools from the bar so we thought we may as well. I covered the seats in red plastic; Otis cleaned up the legs and painted them with chrome paint. When I first moved in, Otis had this old brown velour suit, I just got a load of throws for that, and cushions, neutral colours, tans and wheats, big checks and that, and painted it cream. Then we got this settee after about a year. And then these wooden blinds which I thought, all browns will go with me ornaments, I'm trying to get close to the inside of a pyramid or, like, capture the colours that remind me of Egypt, gold and beige. And this big fan around the light fitting, like it's dead hot. I have in on in the summer, but only on slow or it blows the papyrus scrolls off all our names on the shelf up there. I can hold them down with me turquoise beetle paperweights as I have got three, but what's the point in getting them if I'm gonna have them lay flat. And I don't want them in a frame because then you can't really see the texture, and that's important. We had Charlotte's room painted a light green at first, when it was the nursery, with yellow chiffon curtains up. We didn't want to know what we were having you see. We got a white cot from this girl at work whose baby was now a toddler. It was great except that her lad had gnawed away at the sides when he was teething. But that was fine; I sanded it down and painted over it. But when she grew out of it, we saw this white imitation wrought iron single bed in this furniture shop in Newton Heath. So we got that and got her a couple of beanbags for either side, in case she fell out, which she hasn't yet. And we're gonna paint it pink in there as that's her favourite colour. Our room is a fudge colour, with mirrored fitted wardrobes and a dark brown blind. The bed's like a four-poster and I've wrapped fairy lights round it and in between them I've put little white silk flowers. We've got a long paper lamp in there that me mam got us as a Christmas present. It's shaped like a man, makes Otis jump sometimes. I'm not that keen on that room, might change it this summer, I've never got the bed right, might be better under the window –

BRIDGETTE: Well, I better get back and have a look what I'm going to do –

PAULA: Alright, see you later!

(Sits down and flicks through a magazine.)

ACT ONE, SCENE 4

Bridgette and Ronnie's flat.

Bridgette arrives home and slops down on a chair. Ronnie is screwing something together.

BRIDGETTE: Ahhhhhhhhhh! Why would somebody want to tell you about tiling their bathroom!

RONNIE: I thought you were quickly nipping down to apologise?

BRIDGETTE: I know every nook and cranny of that flat now.

RONNIE: Really, is it nice?

BRIDGETTE: Is it nice? The living room is like the window display of an amusement arcade. Tutankhamen in a tower block, I don't know. I mean, I may be wrong Ronnie, but I'm sure they didn't find gilded tissue boxes in his tomb did they? Or 'Otis loves Paula' in hieroglyphics?

RONNIE: Each to their own my love. We make the best of what we have.

BRIDGETTE: Oh just listen to you. You've already got into the mentality haven't you? Eh? 'Happen we'll make do pet.' At least when Emily and David moved into that council flat they just… kept it neutral, they didn't turn it into a souvenir shop in Cairo. We made the right decision. She'd have died here, on top of a bloody tacky tomb, if we hadn't swapped.

RONNIE: Yes, she wouldn't have liked it.

BRIDGETTE: She couldn't have lived here. She didn't deserve this and you're right, there isn't the time.

RONNIE: I quite like them, they love their daughter.

BRIDGETTE: Well good for them, give them a medal. Of course they love her; she's the only natural thing in there. She's the only thing that's not a bloody plastic imitation of a relic.

RONNIE: I thought you were keen on plastic imitations my love?

BRIDGETTE: Our Venus de Milo water feature is fibre glass, not plastic, you nasty piece of work Ronnie! And that's just practical.

RONNIE: Yes well, the real thing wouldn't have stood the test of time, one stray football from the Garforth's next door... maimed seems to be beautiful, decapitation would have knackered her I suppose.

BRIDGETTE: That house is a testimony to our marriage, our lives. Don't diminish the work you put into that house. We were starting out. We were laughed at when we said we were moving there.

RONNIE: It was a shell of a place.

BRIDGETTE: It wasn't a shell Ronnie; it was a bloody plant pot. You literally couldn't see –

RONNIE: The wood for the trees, yes. You've said dear. At every bloody dinner party or function we've ever been to.

BRIDGETTE: It's a fantastic anecdote 'dear'. Tried and tested many times.

RONNIE: Many times, yes.

BRIDGETTE: My mother said 'He's a bloody chemistry teacher dear. What would he know about renovating a house?' I said –

RONNIE: You said 'If he can't fix it, at least he'll be able to blow it up.'

BRIDGETTE: I didn't say that, I said something much more witty than that... but I can't remember now. Something that would wind up being a fantastic reflection of all the work and care we took of it. Nothing dated, nothing cheap about our place... Why would Emily want to change anything? It's perfect. And... what's the point?

RONNIE: They are attempting to make it their own.

BRIDGETTE: It's not their own.

RONNIE: It is for now.

BRIDGETTE: She must have felt resentment towards the house, that's why. Because... the house will still remain and maybe she wants to destroy it.

RONNIE: She doesn't want to destroy anything.

BRIDGETTE: It's like playing at house. It's a waste of time, getting things, doing it up, just a waste.

RONNIE: Maybe she thinks, well... it's kept us going, it will give her more time... something to concentrate on.

BRIDGETTE: But it's not realistic, it's just a game.

RONNIE: Does it matter?

BRIDGETTE: Yes it fucking matters, it's took us out of the equation... It's like she's making it into a –

RONNIE: She just loves the house, of course she does.

BRIDGETTE: She's making it into a –

RONNIE: There's no point saying things, you're just being silly –

BRIDGETTE: It's a tomb, like heaven downstairs. A bloody tomb with things.

RONNIE: Do you have to chew on every morsel of possibility? Can't you just see the simple equation?

BRIDGETTE: Oh get the chalkboard out why don't you? Let's think logically about the most ludicrous situation ever to happen shall we? I mean, what's the symbol for death on the periodic table Ronnie?

RONNIE: Well, I suppose the closest element would be –

BRIDGETTE: Don't try and be clever! You can't get over this by referencing it in a book. You're going to have to deal with this.

RONNIE: I'll deal with it my way. Then I'll deal with you my way. I'll tend to it, the same way I tended to you, the house and Emily always. In my own flawed and inevitable way.

BRIDGETTE: Two years isn't a long time. It took us that long to turn the garage into the utility room. What a waste of two years.

RONNIE: We could've moved into their council flat and rented.

BRIDGETTE: But HE wanted to make a grand gesture. I wanted him to spend some fucking money. Moving into a fucking five hundred grand dream home, for nothing. I wasn't having that.

RONNIE: Oh yes, and now we're coming round to David.

BRIDGETTE: It's his fault. She's had so many worries with his business. Putting off children, it's too late now... what does a recruitment consultant do?

RONNIE: Now you've got the button.

BRIDGETTE: What does he do that she has to spend hours doing the books for?

RONNIE: You've pushed the button now, here I go –

BRIDGETTE: Go on Ronnie, enjoy yourself.

RONNIE: He takes my daughter and turns an accomplished pianist into an accountant, that's what he does. Tapping away on a computer instead of a piano like she should.

BRIDGETTE: That's right, with all the worries of the world. I hope she has time to do his returns before she goes.

RONNIE: Oh yes, the fucking wet-lipped greedy bastard. Living in a council flat whilst he dines some fucking fat cat he's head-hunted and drives them home in his fucking Beema. I hate that man.

BRIDGETTE: I know you do dear; it's what gets me by.

RONNIE: She hasn't had her hair done in over a year, and there he is with his manicured cheese pealing mitts gesticulating in front of some shithead he's schmoosed. I hate the twat.

BRIDGETTE: I love you for that.

RONNIE: It's not healthy Bridgette. Leave it now.

BRIDGETTE: It's his fault though.

RONNIE: No. It's not his fault. The genes were wrong; it was shit pot luck, that's all. For all his alleged money, he couldn't afford more than a hundred and fifty-grand mortgage though could he?

BRIDGETTE: And there's a retired chemistry teacher with a six-and-a-half-million-pound property.

RONNIE: There is that. I did that for her.

BRIDGETTE: Yes. There's the bottom line. And that's why, although you think I'm a poisonous witch, I made that decision, for you. Everything she has wanted has come from you. From us.

RONNIE: Did you?

BRIDGETTE: Yes, that's why. Because then, he has never replaced us... You.

RONNIE: Maybe you did do it for that reason then.

BRIDGETTE: It used to be that if you didn't study, you'd wind up here, living in a folly with windows. That's what I used to say to my pupils. I'd say as boring as you may find Shakespeare, if you don't read the texts and take note, you'll wind up living in a folly with windows. 'What's a folly, Miss?' It's a monument that the locals would build for something to do, something to get paid for by the Lord of the Manor. Now you're lucky if you can get this. If you can afford a mortgage on a suicide trap, you're doing well. Can't build a place, can't get a dump and do it up. We were lucky.

RONNIE: Otis and what'shername. They won't get to buy anywhere will they? This is temporary for us, remember that. She obviously loves her home, what'shername.

BRIDGETTE: Oh what's the difference anyway, big space, small space. What do we need a load of it for? I'll still have soft furnishings I care for more than you, Ronnie. I'll still have shoes that are more attractive. I just can't figure out why we should stay together, outside of the home.

RONNIE: Give it a month or so, if you still feel the same, we'll sort something out.

BRIDGETTE: Oh give up then you shithead!

(Runs and embraces him.)

Don't do that, just try and figure out what it is that we need each other for will you?

RONNIE: We need each other because everything we built during the past thirty years is slowly falling and we have to protect each other, it's part of the process.

BRIDGETTE: How ridiculous deciding we can't move back! Of course we'll move back. Why did I say that?

RONNIE: I think it's because you felt like you couldn't live there after.

BRIDGETTE: No, I can't! I can't live there after, it's horrible. I won't. I can't bear that. Can't bear the fact that the house she would rather spend her time with, with us out of the picture, will still be there and she'll be gone. Bricks and mortar. No. We can't move back.

RONNIE: Fine.

BRIDGETTE: You'd give all that up! What do you mean fine! It's not fine! This is what she wants! She wants me to feel confused, and useless, like a child. How did I get so removed from her?

RONNIE: Well, I suppose it was when you allowed her to grow up.

BRIDGETTE: I shouldn't have. I wouldn't have, if I'd've known.

RONNIE: I'm going to phone now, and tell her we've settled in and see if she's up to us visiting next week.

BRIDGETTE: Okay.

(Ronnie phones.)

Tell her, that I'm doing well, don't keep asking how she is though. And don't not ask how David is. And ask if she's got any mail for us. Normal things. And see if she wants me to take any shopping round, and ask if there's anything she'd like me to do –

RONNIE: Hello darling –

(Lights down.)

(End of Act One.)

ACT TWO, SCENE 1

At Charlotte's party, which has been in the park across the road.

Otis and Paula sit in the park with party hats on. Paula is holding three party bags. Otis takes a packet of onion rings out of one of them and begins to eat them.

PAULA: Felt like shoving that umbrella up her arse. Following him round with it. Ollie! Ollie! Get under the brolly! Was it raining? They play out in nursery in worse weather. It was a mistake that, inviting every kid in the class. Should've just stuck to the girls. There was no need for that. And it's not because she thinks it's a shit idea having a party in the park. It's because she knows it was a great idea and she didn't think of it for her kid. When I see her on the school run I'm gonna have her. I'm gonna say – sorry Joanne, was Ollie getting wet in the park? Well, bring Ollie's wellies next time.

OTIS: Never mind. Ollies wellies that ends well.

PAULA: She only lives in a terrace you know? It's smaller than our flat by a square metre.

OTIS: It was good, the kids loved it. Bouncy castle.

PAULA: How much is he charging for that?

OTIS: Fifty.

PAULA: See? At Bruntwood Park they charge the kids a quid for ten mins on the bouncy castle. I might tell Joanne it was a hundred instead of fifty.

(Otis rummages through the left-over party bags and finds a little bottle of bubbles. He starts blowing them.)

OTIS: Is there any bubbles in these?

PAULA: Grow up Otis. Anyway, you get the presents. I'll clear up the picnic tables –

OTIS: Oh hang on a minute will you –

PAULA: What, and let some tramp nick her presents? No, come on.

OTIS: Just give it a minute. This is nice. Leave it a bit, your Mam said she'd take the presents back and me Mam said she'd put her to bed.

PAULA: Your Mam took her off pretty quick after the cake.

OTIS: She thought it was going to rain.

PAULA: It's not raining! I checked the forecast when I planned it. If I thought it was gonna rain I'd have bought a marquee.

OTIS: Oh would you now.

PAULA: I don't mean a marquee; I mean one of them skinny ones, like a big shelter thing. Mind you, the bouncy castle wouldn't have worked... I'd've done pass the parcel inside it... The grass might've already been wet, I'd have got some plastic sheeting, mind, that would've been dangerous –

OTIS: It wasn't raining, it was right. It went well. It was a good idea. Stop mithering.

PAULA: We'll have it at the Jolly Jungle next year.

OTIS: Yeah.

PAULA: Charlotte had a good time.

OTIS: Yeah. All her friends there.

PAULA: Yeah. She looked beautiful. Don't start crying again.

OTIS: She is by far the nicest looking kid in that nursery.

PAULA: I really miss her now she's at school. I've lost her to education now. Two years' time, she'll know more about maths than me.

OTIS: Don't be daft.

PAULA: It's very complicated now.

OTIS: Ronnie can help her with her maths.

PAULA: Who?

OTIS: Ronnie upstairs.

PAULA: Oh him. Them two.

OTIS: They're nice people.

PAULA: She avoids me.

OTIS: Does she 'eck.

PAULA: I've seen them, I can count on me hand how many times I've seen them in what? How long? Over a year?

OTIS: Just over a year.

PAULA: She's not said two words to me since she came down to say sorry that day. You know why don't you? She was jealous of our flat. What we've done with it. They were too busy living in a stone mansion in Royston Vasey; they wouldn't have a clue how to make a small space work.

OTIS: It is a bit of a mess in theirs. But it's full of nice mess. Books and paintings. Just a bit cluttered. I'm helping Ronnie put up some shelves.

PAULA: Well you know what Otis? Keeping books, that's pretentious. As Leander says at the Museum, 'Once you've read a book, why put it back on a shelve, it's a waste of space.' Waste of space, that'd be good.

OTIS: Don't start.

PAULA: Can't even have a party in the flat.

OTIS: You could do, but you didn't want to.

PAULA: Because there's no room.

OTIS: Well, we won't always live here.

PAULA: I'd like to live in the Museum.

OTIS: Too cold. I'd like to live in Spain.

PAULA: See you then.

OTIS: You know what we could do? We could buy the flat next door and knock through.

PAULA: You're not allowed to do that.

OTIS: Whose gonna know. Right, we could keep the two front doors and just knock it through, like a penthouse.

PAULA: A penthouse, quite fancy that, yeah. But it's not for sale though is it? Oh, it's alright, it's a nice place, best view in town, it's just that I'd like her to have a garden.

OTIS: I'd like her to have a lot of things, but that's life. At least we have a good holiday. Get to see the world.

PAULA: I feel dead free when I'm away. In the sea, on the sand, Char can roam free.

OTIS: Shall we try somewhere different this year?

PAULA: No, we're going back to Egypt.

OTIS: It's too hot.

PAULA: Don't come then.

OTIS: You love it there don't you?

PAULA: Yeah, I do. Remember that day when you took Char out on the camels and I stayed at the hotel? You know how you're always saying like, take your top off, everyone else does? Well, I did. I took it off and I went in the sea. Felt really good actually.

OTIS: Why didn't you do it when I was there? That was the point!

PAULA: It was great. They were, like, weightless. I felt dead brave and like a fish, all the ocean was mine. Well, got cold after a bit and had to prepare myself to get out, I was worried that everyone would be looking at me, but they weren't, we were all just there, being how we wanted to be. I felt massive, but I felt part of everything. I didn't go back to the sunbed, I walked down the beach, dead confident.

OTIS: I wish I'd have seen that.

PAULA: No, it was just about me, and space, freedom. Yeah, it was lovely. I saw these kids playing volleyball and I couldn't help meself, just ran over and joined in. They were all laughing, think they got me vibe you know.

OTIS: Did you?

PAULA: Yeah, played for about ten minutes, loads of people came and joined in. I felt so daring, jumping around, diving about... wore meself out after a bit and walked back to the sunbed.

OTIS: And put your top on?

PAULA: I got me purse and went to the bar, sat there and had a beer and a pizza, I sat with them blokes from Newcastle, remember them? Dead friendly? I had a good laugh with them. Finished me pizza, gave them all a big hug, went back to the sunbed. Imagining it was my beach, my place.

OTIS: But you had your top on though, didn't you?

PAULA: Eh? No, I don't want to go anywhere else, maybe I wouldn't enjoy it as much, I don't want to risk it, we're happy there, we know we'll have a good time.

(Otis gets a phone call.)

OTIS: Hello? Alright Ronnie, yeah... erm, yeah okay... I don't really know that area, but... yeah, they can direct me can't they. Okay mate, just give us about fifteen minutes, alright, yeah, see you later, ta-ra. Ronnie. He wanted to know if I could drive Emily and David back, he had one too many and forgot he was taking them.

PAULA: Who are they?

OTIS: His daughter and her husband, they've been round for their dinner and he forgot he was taking them back.

PAULA: Oh right. Are you taking them?

OTIS: Yeah. I wonder how bad she is; she didn't have long did she? Even when they moved in, she didn't have long.

PAULA: Aye, you'll get to see their house won't you? The Beautiful House. Tell me all about it.

OTIS: I will, I'll have a good nosey. Try and take some pictures on me phone to show you.

ACT TWO, SCENE 2

Otis returns to the flat from dropping Emily and David and we hear the door shut.

Paula is eating some birthday cake on the settee watching telly; the room is quiet and cosy.

PAULA: Well, what's it like? Did you take any pictures?

OTIS: No.

PAULA: Well? Go on?

OTIS: She's very ill you know.

PAULA: Is she?

OTIS: She doesn't have long, it's bad. Never seen that before. Maybe Ronnie couldn't face dropping them back. She said that Ronnie thought a lot of me, can you believe that? She's had enough, I think. It doesn't seem fair.

PAULA: What's... the house like?

OTIS: Paula, are you listening to me, I'm telling you about a woman, their daughter nearly gone. Every breath like this – like... like if she didn't bother once, that would be it.

PAULA: That's sad. It is sad that. I'm glad I didn't see her. Did you go in the house?

OTIS: Yeah. I helped him get her inside. She's nice.

PAULA: What's the house like?

(There is a knock at the door and Otis goes to answer. It is Ronnie and Bridgette, in high spirits. Ronnie has a good look around the living room and shares a joke with Bridgette about how dreadful it is.)

BRIDGETTE: Hello!

PAULA: Hello, nice to see you again. It's Charlotte's birthday today; do you want a piece of cake?

BRIDGETTE: Oh, no thank you.

RONNIE: No we've eaten enough. You had a party in the park didn't you?

BRIDGETTE: Oh, how lovely. I hope the rain didn't spoil it.

PAULA: It's not been raining.

BRIDGETTE: Oh, I thought I saw a few droplets earlier. Okay. Did they get back okay?

OTIS: Fine, yeah. She was fine. Do you want a drink of anything?

BRIDGETTE: No we're fine. Fine.

(Ronnie and Bridgette are giggling.)

Paula, do you still have that picture that changes, that one of Tutankhamen?

PAULA: Yeah, yeah, it's here –

BRIDGETTE: Show it to Ronnie, look Ronnie. *(Grabs it.)* Ronnie look – it goes from the sarcophagus to the mummy, look. *(Begins to laugh.)*

PAULA: It is meant to be funny.

RONNIE: Oh, that's wonderful, yes. Bit spooky.

OTIS: Emily gave me this to give you Ronnie. She said to open it after she'd died.

(Laughing stops dead.)

PAULA: Did she have a good time today? Emily?

BRIDGETTE: Let me see, let... let me.

RONNIE: You won't open it! No! I'm keeping it safe, thank you. Come on now. Thank you for taking her home Otis, thank you. Good night.

[Exits.]

BRIDGETTE: *[Exiting.]* Let me see it Ronnie! Just let me have a look at it!

OTIS: But she told me to say that and to try and catch them when they were chirpy.

PAULA: What's it like then anyway? Come on?

OTIS: It's a grey building, detached, bit like a vicarage. Lead windows.

PAULA: Like your Mam's?

(During the following, Otis exits but is heard offstage. Within that time, Paula shows how in awe she is of the description, becomes overwhelmed with yearning, then pretends to be nonchalant when Otis re-enters.)

OTIS: No, real. Catching the light, like. Big garden all the way round, big windows. Big red front door with frosted glass and a brass knob. On the side, the windows go round the corner at the bottom, like turrets but on the upstairs looking at it, from the right, there's a wooden balcony with a wooden trellis like above. Those windows are stained glass. Bet it was a vicarage. There's a big oak tree in the front garden, two paths leading either side to the back. It's set back from the road and then elevated, them steps are a bit steep for her now I think. Inside it's like exposed brick or plastered, painted dark red or green. Bit festive I suppose, big fire in the middle of the living room, have you seen one of them? Do you know what I mean? Like a lodge or something. There's carpet in there but mostly wooden creaky floorboards, corridors and flags in big spaces, like the dining room and kitchen. Big Aga in the kitchen, pans and herbs hanging from the ceiling. Big exposed old sink, massive. Long oak table. Wrought iron light fittings everywhere. It's like some inn Dick Turpin would go to, like Shambles Square must've been, like that. 'Cept they've got a big plasma screen telly, like ours, but massive. Part from that, it was all, you know, brickwork and dark and regal, kind of, you know, countrified.

PAULA: Is that what it was like?

OTIS: Yeah.

PAULA: Eughhhhhhh!

OTIS: What d'you mean?

PAULA: Oh no, I don't like that. Sounds all cold and spooky. Sounds like the Addams Family!

OTIS: Well, it was night time. I loved it.

PAULA: Oh it's made me shiver that. Like when we went and did that murder mystery at work and people were strangled to death. Everyone was laughing, remember I told you? They were all getting into it, I hated it. I was ready to literally kill that fella, I got too involved. Gave me this little card saying 'you are going to die'. I grabbed his balls. I said 'You are, you are, you are.' Couldn't stop saying it, I was terrified. I see him now and again at the Museum, he plays a Viking in this re-enactment they do. I can't look him in the face. That place was like that. All green lamps and brasses on the walls.

OTIS: She said some things, Emily. Said some things to me, her husband was a bit shocked.

PAULA: Oh aye?!

OTIS: No, not like that. Oh, she was probably just being kind, but then David said, actually, that's a wonderful idea. I just said, now come on you two, don't be silly, and went. It was nice to meet her, never seen anyone like that before and she was sort of, don't know, gracious with it, she was... she's a lovely girl. Seemed very genuine, honest. You know what Paul, eh? I think things are gonna change for us, for the better, in the long run. Wait and see baby.

ACT TWO, SCENE 3

Emily has died.

It is late and Bridgette and Ronnie have returned to the house.

BRIDGETTE: I told those nurses Ronnie. I said 'Don't you dare come to work here tomorrow. Don't you dare carry on with this as if it's just a job, after this. Seeing my little girl go.' I hate them, how everything carries on... I would like to have some things from the house. Just some clothes and some things. I would like to have her rings. David wouldn't want them, would he love? Ronnie, I'm okay if you want to leave now, but you have to put things in place, be in control now Ronnie, it's time now, take control, now. Ronnie? We have to get on now... She fought to the last second, and I think she did it because she thought we'd come up with something... I think you had something in mind but didn't say and you've fucking ruined it now. Make her come back baby, get her back now my love, get my baby, find her, bring her back to me now! Why can't you make things okay now? Why can't you fucking change things? You can just fuck off and die then, if you can't. Why would I want to carry on with you if you can't do that one thing and... why can't you, you... bring her back and change things you bastard! You're so good at things, come on then! She doesn't deserve this!

RONNIE: I'm so tired. If I had the energy and inclination I would throttle you, I really would. You're so selfish, Bridgette. So selfish and stupid. I really feel like I've lost the one person in the world that knows and loves me. She really loved me. Without doubt. And I loved her. Come home, have a meal, read the papers, talk to my daughter about her day-to-day. I love her more than I... she is love, life, I'm only going to carry on if you want me to Bridgette, if you don't I won't.

RONNIE: When's David coming back?

BRIDGETTE: I don't know, when he's ready I suppose, he has things to fill in there. When shall we look at the letter?

RONNIE: In a minute. Do you want a bath?

BRIDGETTE: No.

RONNIE: Have something to eat.

BRIDGETTE: I don't want anything –

RONNIE: Get out of the room Bridgette.

BRIDGETTE: I don't want to get out –

RONNIE: I need to be alone in here.

BRIDGETTE: I can't leave you, not right now.

RONNIE: I want to do something, and I don't want you to watch me, okay?

BRIDGETTE: I won't watch you –

RONNIE: I want to do something –

BRIDGETTE: Just do it Ronnie, I'm not going to watch you –

(Ronnie goes and sits down on the settee, smells it, then hugs it. He is devastated. Bridgette turns to look.)

Ronnie... darling... I need to tell you something...

RONNIE: Oh just leave me to it will you? Just leave me to it please!

I want to smell her, I want to hug her. I'm sorry Emily, I'm so sorry Emily.

BRIDGETTE: Ronnie…

RONNIE: Oh what is it you selfish bitch!

BRIDGETTE: She never sat there Ronnie… that's where David sits. *(Begins to laugh.)* You idiot!

RONNIE: It's not where David sits; it's where she used to lie down.

BRIDGETTE: No… no, it was too soft for her; she sat on the chair there, with the pouf. David slouches on the sofa in his boxers, scratching his nuts. She told me.

RONNIE: Yes, sat scratching his fucking nuts whilst my daughter is leaving, leaving. I don't know how to get round this.

BRIDGETTE: Are you ready for the letter?

RONNIE: I'm not ready for anything, I wasn't ready for today and I would never have been ready.

BRIDGETTE: Well, I'm going to look at some things now.

RONNIE: Don't touch anything.

BRIDGETTE: I can touch what I fucking like, she's my fucking baby! I want to get her coat.

(Bridgette brings in her coat, she clutches it to her.)

Now then, this smells of my baby.

(Ronnie goes to grab it and Bridgette runs out of his grasp. He pursues her and they grapple with the coat until they are both clutching it very tightly. There should be a lot of crying and emotions getting to the surface without self-awareness, but guttural screaming and crying and grappling.)

(Lights down.)

(Lights up.)

(They are now on the sofa clutching the coat, tired and are exhausted by their emotions and have clearly been crying a lot.)

RONNIE: Where's the letter?

BRIDGETTE: You have it.

(Ronnie reaches into his pocket and produces a beautiful envelope with a seal on the back. They open it together and Ronnie holds the letter from Emily. He gathers himself.)

RONNIE: *(Reads.)* 'Dad.'

BRIDGETTE: Oh it's just to you is it? Right.

RONNIE: 'And before you say anything Mum, there is a section for you, just be patient, if I started with your section you would be indulging in your own grief whilst Dad read his section out, so, listen to Dad's bit first, okay?'

BRIDGETTE: If I must.

RONNIE: 'Dad, just want to say thank you. Thanks for tolerating David, I know you hate him. And although I am the best pianist in the world, I would rather be a number-cruncher for David, because I love him and believe in him. I only played the piano for you Dad, in actual fact; I'm not very keen on it. If it makes you feel any better, if it hadn't been for the deadly lumps, between the piano playing for you, and the computer keyboard for David, my hands would be crippled with arthritis by the time I was forty. David has loved and cared for me, as much as you. I have felt your love all my life. You were there at the beginning, you will be there at the end, what more could a daughter ask for? Look after Mum and don't try and find me, I'll have gone and there's no point looking. By the end, I won't be fighting, I'll be relieved. Life is as short as long. Remember our happy times and be assured you definitely did your very best. Mum, as you know, I've never been very fond of you. I've always felt like I was a poor substitute for your musical career. And I never told Dad about your alleged affair with David Essex, as I always knew this was a lie to impress me.'

BRIDGETTE: True.

RONNIE: 'It's hard to believe you ever made a penny out of singing, since you are as flat as my lungs are slowly becoming, but we indulge you. It's a good job you are the most beautiful and charismatic women a man could ever meet or I would probably never have existed, so I thank you for that. I have thoroughly enjoyed taking over the house, for all the reasons you imagine. But most of all, because you became my daughter. And I imagine a daughter of mine would be very much like you. And through that process I've seen you in a different light. I've seen you as a little girl who needs a lot of looking after, a process I imagine I would have gone through if I'd have had to watch you die. The dying are very philosophical, so, here I go – things are things. I don't give a shit about the house; I would've lived in a shed if it meant I could live. Things are nothing. The intangible is mettle of memories and life's little affirmations. This house will be here whether we are or not, so will that flat you hate so much. They're nothing but what we define them to be. I was the investment, I was the nurtured thing, me. The last thing I will ever know is you kissing me goodbye, you wonderful, awful, beautiful woman. I am writing this last bit just after Otis has drove us home, what a lovely man! Loves his wife and daughter, reminds me of you, Dad. I am giving him this letter to give you, and I want you to think very carefully about...'

(Ronnie reads the rest to himself, then gives it to Bridgette who embraces him.)

BRIDGETTE: She'll have spoken to him about it. It's one last thing to get at me.

RONNIE: We'll see if she did. Silly girl. It's not fair to do that, to expect us to... and to hurt the man's feelings. She didn't want us to have an easy ride did she? You're right; she must've really resented this house. But she was wrong, it was never loved as much as her, never will be. And she hasn't done this to hurt you Bridgette, this is for my benefit. And I will see this through.

ACT TWO, SCENE 4

Ronnie has invited Otis over and sits nervously waiting for the door.

RONNIE: *(Shouts.)* Come in, it's open!

(Otis enters, exhilarated, nearly fit to burst. He runs over and hugs Ronnie.)

OTIS: How are you? I'm so sorry Ronnie. We thought it was best just to leave you alone... and just let you get on with it, you know. I'm so sorry mate.

RONNIE: Well, terrible as you can imagine, but we're getting on with it. It's bad, for both of us.

OTIS: Did you get our card? I know I only met her once, but I really liked her, she was such a nice person.

RONNIE: Thank you, thank you... sit down, if you would, I have something to tell you.

OTIS: Oh, I can't sit down Ronnie.

RONNIE: Please, I have something to tell you –

OTIS: You see, I kind of guessed, you see from what Emily said to me that day I dropped her off. I can't believe she actually did it.

RONNIE: So... Emily spoke to you about this, did she?

OTIS: I didn't take it as read Ronnie, I didn't dare imagine Ronnie.

RONNIE: I think it was a lovely idea.

OTIS: I don't believe it! I just can't believe it!

(Embraces him.)

Oh thank you Ronnie! Thank you so much! It's like a dream, things like this, they never happen.

RONNIE: Yes.

OTIS: Where's Bridgette? I want everyone together when I tell Paula!

RONNIE: She's just gone for a little walk in the park, she shouldn't be long.

OTIS: Oh I'll wait on then. I'm climbing out of me skin me.

RONNIE: Well, it certainly will make a big difference to your life.

OTIS: Like you wouldn't believe! You know, I've always fucking hated it here, but I didn't want Paula to know, I didn't want her to know, didn't want to upset her. I'm gonna make her fucking year, never mind day! Oh, Ronnie, I hate it round here, the piss-stinking lift, the cold wind whistling through the windows, the fucking kids below with fuck all to do but smash the office window. That won't be Charlotte now, will it eh, Ronnie?

RONNIE: I suppose it could change things for the better –

OTIS: She's not going to believe this, Paul. I mean, I said to her after that night, I said I think things will change for the better but I didn't say owt. I couldn't do it, you know, in case it didn't happen, I couldn't do that to her. She doesn't know this, but I've always want to live in the country –

RONNIE: I'm sure it would certainly help, as a deposit for a mortgage, yes –

OTIS: What –

RONNIE: It is certainly a generous amount.

OTIS: What?

RONNIE: The money that Emily left for you. The two thousand pound she left for you? I think she was very struck with you Otis, and I am not surprised. She said in her letter she was struck by how fond you were of your daughter and your wife and felt she wanted to give you something. She was a very kind, thoughtful girl.

OTIS: Yeah... That's... very kind of her.

RONNIE: So, hey, David is selling this flat when we move back to our... house, so, maybe you could put it toward a deposit for this place, or... another trip to Egypt...

OTIS: Yeah, okay Ronnie. I understand.

RONNIE: So, I'll give you the cheque now, from my account, it's easier and then... it's done. Just in case we don't see you again, we'll be busy packing this next week or so...

OTIS: If you want to give me two grand from your account, that's fine by me Ronnie. Fine by me. It's your decision.

RONNIE: It's fine, it's... I can sort it out with David.

OTIS: Yeah, you do that. It's not every day you get a load of money from a kind person who saw you were a good person, now is it?

RONNIE: She was a lovely person, kind –

OTIS: I had a good chat with her; she thought the world of you.

RONNIE: I felt the same –

OTIS: She said you always did right by her. You always knew what was best.

RONNIE: Yes. I've always done what's best for my family.

OTIS: I didn't expect anything, didn't dwell on it, it was too big a thing.

RONNIE: You have to understand, Emily was very ill.

OTIS: Oh, I don't want your house Ronnie! And I don't want your money; I just want you to be honest.

RONNIE: Now, let's not make this –

OTIS: Ronnie, I know what Emily said, and that was your daughter and she was right. She thought it would make you happy to give us a chance in life, one that she couldn't have, she wanted me and Paul and Char to have that.

RONNIE: You only met her once.

OTIS: And that was enough for her. How can you do that to us Ronnie? Eh? It's so cruel. You said you wished us all that we could get from life; you said you wished Charlotte everything Emily has had.

RONNIE: I meant the torture, the utter torture and pain! You've no idea about cruelty and pain. Try watching the life fade out of your daughter's eyes, you'll never forget that.

OTIS: Ronnie, you're a good man you don't mean that.

RONNIE: I mean every word!

OTIS: Now Ronnie –

RONNIE: How dare you ask me for my home. Emily would not in her right mind have promised our house to you. It wasn't hers to give. You must understand, she wasn't thinking clearly –

OTIS: Why would you fucking deserve it eh? What you gonna do now, eh? Sit there, fucking festering in grief. You don't deserve it; you've got no life left now. Look at us, stuck here in a fucking box. It's not fair. You should do the right thing.

RONNIE: You've got no fucking claim on our life! You fucking pestered my daughter didn't you? When she wasn't well enough to make the decision for herself, you twisted her arm when she was ill. You're despicable!

OTIS: No Ronnie. I didn't say anything to her or David. We sat and had a brew, we talked about... we talked about you and Bridgette, David took us round the house. That was that.

RONNIE: You're a manipulative bully!

OTIS: You're wrong Ronnie. I'm not, I just want to live somewhere nice with me family and it hurts me I can't. But you can paint me anyway you like, I know I'm not like that. I can make the most of my life here. I've got me family. It's more than you've got. It's all you've got, that house. Here y'are, keep your cheque.

(Bridgette enters from the bedroom.)

BRIDGETTE: What Emily said in the letter –

RONNIE: She said to give them something we thought they deserved.

BRIDGETTE: She meant the house.

RONNIE: It wasn't Emily's to give and it certainly isn't now –

BRIDGETTE: They might think we were trying to hurt them.

RONNIE: They can think what they like. I've done everything she wanted, everything for her, and she's not here now Bridgette, she's just not here. Do you think, I would have ever given up the house? I'm not giving it up, we can build something back there again, not here. You know what this is Bridgette? It's called not letting the crap control me. We moved here on a whim, we are not going to lose our home on another whim from Emily. It would be lovely if people did things like that, but that's not how the world works. The world isn't a lovely place, not now. I thought it was, but then it shat on me. And I expected too much of her. To love someone that much and expect them to be better than yourself, it wasn't fair. So, she put me in a position where I could have changed a person's life for the better. And she gave me the choice, and I haven't taken it. I'm not that good after all.

ACT TWO, SCENE 5

Otis and Paula's flat.

Paula enters with a coat and umbrella. Otis is looking out of the window, upset.

PAULA: I've forgotten it's dancing after school. So you'll have to run up in a bit with the tap shoes. Another party invitation. That'll be two in the same week, Sat 22nd and Sun 23rd. She's a right what-they-called, what are they called, party animal, no, socialite, yeah. Daisy's talking to her again. They were linking going into class. So we can sleep at night again now, the friendship's back on. What you doing gawping out the window, you weirdo.

OTIS: Something horrible's happened.

PAULA: Has your Mum died?

OTIS: No.

PAULA: Has my Mum died???!!!

OTIS: No. It's not like that.

PAULA: Well, it can't be that bad then. Has the car been nicked?

OTIS: The dream's been nicked.

PAULA: What dream?

OTIS: We nearly had something, and he stole it. I should've got her to write it down for me, sign something. No I shouldn't, I wouldn't have done that.

PAULA: What you going on about?

OTIS: Ronnie, he's fucking ripped us off!

PAULA: How?

OTIS: His daughter, wanted to leave the house to us –

PAULA: Us? Me and you? She didn't even know us –

OTIS: And he pretended she wanted us to have two grand –

PAULA: Two grand! Fucking hell, where is it?

OTIS: I told him to shove it.

PAULA: You what? Fucking get down there now. Right, we're going to Egypt for Christmas.

(Gets out brochures.)

What you waiting for? Get downstairs and say sorry.

OTIS: I'm not sorry, he should be sorry, he lied to me. I know she wanted us to have the house, she told me. She said that we deserved to bring a child up in that house, just like she'd been.

PAULA: She was... dying want she? It's their house, they'll be moving back now.

OTIS: They are. But, I don't want their house, I wanted him to say, to say that it was what she wanted, instead of fobbing us off out of his own pocket.

PAULA: Eh, what am I on about, Egypt; we could put a deposit down on their flat.

OTIS: Why the fuck would we do that?

PAULA: We could actually own a flat then.

OTIS: What difference will that make?

PAULA: Well, couple of years' time, we could sell it and get a bigger place.

OTIS: We nearly had a massive fucking house in the country.

PAULA: Did we 'eck! It's their home Otis. She was just staying there for... a bit.

OTIS: I wanted it to be a surprise for you, he saw how chuffed I was, bastard. We deserve that house, that's what she said. I saw it, Charlotte would love it there, she'd go to a good school with lovely kids. Well-spoken and kind. A village, lovely scenery, river nearby. I worked out the journey to work, less than an hour it is. Big tree at Christmas. Christmas lights in the oak tree in the garden. What a lovely place to grow up. I can't bear it. I felt like it was going to happen. And he could see it in my eyes. Then there's them two, moving back, to mourn her. What's the point in us trying to get that flat Paul? It's part of this it's not on its own.

PAULA: It's their home Otis; they've lived there longer than I've been alive. Listen babe, I'd live in a cave if it meant being with you. I know you only married me for me knockers, but you mean the absolute world to me. And if that world is this tower block and two weeks in Egypt a year, fine by me. That's all I need.

OTIS: How much do you love me?

PAULA: Put it this way, if you ever tried to have an affair, I'd axe you to death. That's how much.

OTIS: Right, I know we could've done with that two grand but I couldn't take his money.

PAULA: It wouldn't have been right to take it. Anyway, I'm glad to see the back of them... see who moves in next –

OTIS: Well I'm not getting to know them.

PAULA: Don't be horrible. You know what they say at the Tenants' Association? They say 'Why live in the country when you can live in a vertical village with the best views in the city.'

OTIS: What are they gonna say though Paul eh? It's shit here?

PAULA: I can't believe you were that daft to think that would happen. As if they would've...

OTIS: Yeah.

PAULA: It's too far for work anyway, we spend half the time in the car, then there's schools. Anyway, shut up, why am I even entertaining it?

OTIS: If I'm ever given an opportunity to make a better life for us three, I'm gonna grab it with both hands every time, don't ever expect me to be any different will you? That's what I'm like! I don't care what anyone thinks. How long we gonna be here anyway? All these David types are buying them up. The council are selling everything off. What's worse than this eh? That's what's waiting round the corner for us. And he knows that, Ronnie. It's our lives! We're just a little dirty mark on the skyline that they're gonna rub out. They'll knock down the tower block and build a bigger one with less room inside. They'll stop calling them flats and start calling them apartments, for people with... lifestyles. It's not ours Paul. It's just a big monument and we're like a load of... fucking scarab ants, picking away at a life inside it, but it doesn't belong to them. We very nearly had something there.

PAULA: Beetles. Scarab beetles we are, not ants.

(The noise of the flats and from the street outside can be heard as the lights fade.)

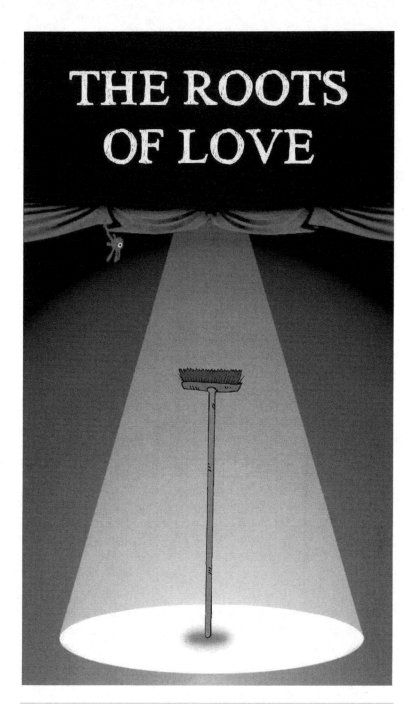

Premiered at Studio Salford, 2010

"This story is influenced and inspired by 'What Becomes of the Broken Hearted' by Jimmy Ruffin. That song is approximately four minutes long and yet resonates beyond the time, the era, and the original sentiment, to give a universal feel of sorrow, and longing, and love, and despair. This play is around forty minutes long and the intention is the same. At the end of the play, during the last few seconds of action, I would like the song played and the lights lifted to the highest possible brightness whilst the song belts out. It should be the song that has the last word on the subject, as it is the song that has driven the whole play." *CC*

CAST (2)

LEN

Aged around 50 years old. Since Len has no idea or consideration for the fact that he has immense charisma, he is attractive and endearing to most people. Sorrow and booze have been his mates for a very long time though; they are his best mates, but they're not his only mates. He is a great teller of stories. They aren't wonderful, but whatever he tells you, you are instantly engaged in. He is wise and has lifted the veil to life and worked it all out. He can interact with flair and is open and understanding to others, and would not let anyone feel uncomfortable about anything they wanted to do with their life. He feels he needs to covet Fran as she has become like a commodity to him, despite the fact he would much prefer her as a friend. And, although he cannot bear to admit it, as the mother of his child. A broken heart did his back in. A broken heart made him unable to work again. Though he has daughters that love him very much, he hasn't been able to reach down to the part that loved them absolutely since he lost Mikey. He thinks he gets away with this by loving them as much as he can muster. Len will realise he has lost two loves of his life and yet will still only ever and forever mourn one.

FRAN

Fran is in her late 30s. She has been robbed of certain things at a young age, meaning that she had no gauge on how to transcend from child to adult. She has eyes that greet the world with passion and enthusiasm, as she has only known to be grateful for life and not to take it for granted. She still plays netball for a team that have been playing together at Sunday League for ten years. She will beat everyone at board games and feel bad about it. She paints portraits for her friend's families of their kids. She would give you her last fiver. Her wife, Sarah, has the flesh of her charred heart and she looks after it as well as anyone could. The new baby has been bittersweet. Fran's imagination knows no bounds and she should have been a writer, but it has been directed into a form of soothing for Len which seems relentless – and results in her feeling barren and used. She wanted it to mean that Len would forgive her; it never did. Now Fran knows she must bury the past and say goodbye. She has a wife and a new baby, and she knows she deserves this. She knows she has paid her dues. But she doesn't know whether it will all work out. She has no self-pity and has carried guilt as barbed wire around her heart. The only time she has ever allowed herself to feel the sadness she, as a mother of a lost child deserved, is her parting speech.

SCENE 1

The song 'Helpless' by Kim Weston is played as the lights come up on a living room covered in dust sheets.

As Len makes a roll-up, Fran is cleaning her hands with a rag – she has just finished whitewashing Len's house.

FRAN: It's going well int it, nice, going well, lovely...

LEN: You done a great job there Franny. You've elevated yourself in my estimation, as you've lifted the colour of me walls and brightened my cave.

FRAN: I've only whitewashed the walls mate, steady on there.

LEN: I've got a bit windy you know now, over ladders.

FRAN: You nearly did a Rod Hull didn't you mate that time?

LEN: I fucking did yeah. Bastard council should've done that not me.

FRAN: They won't touch satellite dishes Len. You got to get Sky to do that.

LEN: I'm not arsed anyway, it's down now so... stops me watching it and not doing me reading. Books, that's what feeds the imagination Fran.

FRAN: Oh I know.

LEN: Reading, that's food for thought, and better than anything you see on that crap machine.

FRAN: Yeah I know Len, I like reading. Bugs Sarah a bit, she goes 'Turn that light off Franbo, it'll wake her up.'

LEN: Haha-haha-hah, Franbo, ha-aha-haha, is that what she calls you?!

FRAN: I've always been Fran haven't I? Or well... Franny. She doesn't like Franny.

LEN: Anyway, get the brews on, get the brandy out of the biscuit cupboard. Thought you'd never ask...

(Fran exits.)

FRAN: *(Offstage.)* So who's this Pat then?

LEN: Pat, yeah, she's alright, her kids are arseholes but, she doesn't see them much, whether it's by choice or not I don't know. She's got two lads and two girls. I say girls, they all seem to be thirty, but that can't be right.

FRAN: What's she like?

LEN: Nice... she works at the Co-op on the deli counter, blonde hair, big tits.

FRAN: What more do you want?

LEN: Well yeah, she won't let me upstairs though, we have to do it on the sofa. Dog was licking me arsehole last Saturday... quite nice...

FRAN: I was gonna say, bonus.

LEN: I mean, what the fuck difference does it make? If any of them walked in, which they won't because she never sees them, that would be worse wouldn't it?

FRAN: Speaking of kids –

LEN: Ah don't show me baby pictures –

FRAN: I've only got a couple, two secs –

(Fran's face lights up and she gets out her phone to show Len. Various noises and comments ensue over whichever one they are looking at, their faces change expression at the same time, to the end one which is the birth that Fran has filmed on the phone. There is a look of shock and Fran turns it off.)

Sorry Len! Sorry, I thought I'd moved that to me laptop.

LEN: Jesus! ... Jesus! You could've warned me! Ohhh me hands have gone all tingly now.

FRAN: Sorry Len.

LEN: What did you film that for?

FRAN: Well I did it for me Mam.

LEN: Your Mam wanted to see that?!

FRAN: Well, no, what it was, was that Sarah didn't want me Mam in there, and so I filmed it for her. I cut out that bit when I sent it me Mam, just shown her when she did her first cry.

LEN: Why keep that though? Isn't it gonna put you off?

FRAN: I was just like, you know. Overwhelmed.

LEN: It's not right that Fran. Anyway, it's up to you. How do you feel then?

(Pours them another brandy.)

FRAN: I feel, charged and big. I feel like all the world is clinging to me all of a sudden.

LEN: Eh?

FRAN: She's so beautiful.

LEN: Is she balls!

FRAN: Ahh she is, these pictures don't do her justice.

LEN: She looks like Churchill, like the all do.

FRAN: No, Len. She's beautiful.

LEN: They all look the same.

FRAN: My daughter is beautiful Len. She is.

LEN: Alright I know. So's mine, so's everyone's.

FRAN: How is Dawn?

LEN: Ahh she's fine. Great.

FRAN: How's Katie?

LEN: There great you know, fine, doing alright.

FRAN: No sign of grandkids yet then?

LEN: Well... nah I don't think so.

FRAN: Be good for you that.

LEN: Joking aren't you?

FRAN: Some children here, that would brighten the place up.

LEN: What was it Mikey called you –

FRAN: Mumum.

LEN: Do you know what popped into my head the other day? I don't know why – his third birthday... we went swimming, remember?

FRAN: No... don't remember that, you sure I was there?

LEN: Probably not, no.

FRAN: No wonder I don't remember it then.

LEN: Yeah, took him swimming, that's when he got the taste for it.

FRAN: He loved swimming, yeah.

LEN: It was me that first called you Franny.

FRAN: Oh I don't know about that Len, I'll have to ask me Mam.

LEN: She'll tell you! It was me that called it you. You always wanted to call him Sunbun and he wouldn't let you.

FRAN: I thought he loved Sunbun, thought he let me.

(Pause.)

(They have another drink and calmness enters the room.)

LEN: It'll be the making of you this.

FRAN: I hope so.

LEN: Oh yeah. You'll love having a daughter. A daughter eh?

FRAN: I know.

LEN: Do you know what I was gonna do? And this will surprise you. I was thinking that you could do the ceiling.

FRAN: I can't really –

LEN: No, I mean in a minute, later. I'm taking the alien down.

FRAN: Are you?

LEN: That's how I am now Fran, I'm ready.

FRAN: I'm sure I threw that up anyway.

LEN: No you didn't, did you balls.

FRAN: Oh right.

LEN: Mikey did that, you weren't even here.

FRAN: Probably not, no.

LEN: There's was only me and him here.

FRAN: Are you sure?

LEN: And it was a Sunday, you were out with your Dad.

FRAN: Yeah, fucking beer garden somewhere me on Sundays.

LEN: Look, I know things are different now you've had the baby –

FRAN: It's just –

LEN: And I know it can't, you know you... well you have to move on –

FRAN: It's not that I don't care –

LEN: But I just want to say, let it go Fran –

FRAN: Let it go?

LEN: All this about not being here – it's silly –

FRAN: Silly?

LEN: It's daft you thinking like that –

FRAN: I wasn't talking about that –

LEN: Well it's daft –

FRAN: At all. I wasn't talking about that, I was just saying, that's where I would have been on a Sunday.

LEN: Am I not allowed to say something? Can I just say something, please Fran.

FRAN: Fine. Yeah.

LEN: You were very young. And I've never said that before have I?

FRAN: I don't think badly of you. I've never done –

LEN: I'm not talking about that! That was you all that, you cheeky sod! I mean to have been expected to act like a mum.

FRAN: Oh right. Yeah. I know.

LEN: You didn't know what to do.

FRAN: I'll always be grateful Len.

LEN: You didn't have a clue.

FRAN: Like you say, I was a kid, you were more like a big brother really.

LEN: I remember it, he'd had it two minutes. The alien.

FRAN: I'll always be grateful, you know that.

LEN: He'd only had it two minutes, think it was in some kind of lucky bag.

FRAN: *(Starts to appear visibly defeated.)* Was it?

LEN: Yeah, from Papa's off licence it was.

FRAN: Yeah, it was. I remember now.

LEN: See?

FRAN: Yeah. It was a Swizzles lucky bag. You got two drumsticks. Some fruit salads. A small comic. Tattoos and an alien.

LEN: Dawn got hers to slide down the wall but –

FRAN: Mikey threw his up on the ceiling and it stuck there.

LEN: Mikey was upset and she gave him hers.

FRAN: And he made it walk down the window, but I went mad.

LEN: And threw it in the bin.

FRAN: And you went to get it out and it had all hair stuck on it from –

LEN: From Katie's brush, and fluff that wouldn't come off.

FRAN: And Mikey was laughing, saying it had grown up –

LEN: Hahaha yeah, he did.

FRAN: And grown a beard –

LEN: Yeah, he said it needed a shave didn't he? And you said it was a scruffy bastard like me –

FRAN: You didn't like that at the time.

LEN: Except that we shouldn't say Mikey, because we said, didn't we, he'd be Michael now and we wouldn't say that in his company would we? As a grown man –

FRAN: We're not talking about him as a grown man.

LEN: I wasn't doing that.

FRAN: We don't know what he would or wouldn't –

LEN: The alien's real, that's what happened.

FRAN: And then you started...

LEN: Let's get him down, eh? He's been up there long enough. Go and get me yard brush.

(Len walks around and stares straight above him, looking panicked.)

(Fran comes back in with the yard brush – Len will use the handle end because he won't want to ruin it. Len gets up and teeters on the chair.)

I don't want to do the table, it's not safe.

FRAN: I can get up there.

LEN: No, I'm doing it... you just grab me.

(Fran and Len clasp hands as Len reaches out for and tries to knock or scrape the 'alien' down – in reality, a sticky wall crawler toy. It looks like a ballet. He flicks it and then runs off in a direction it has landed.)

(Len moves over to Fran in a solemn fashion and stares and strokes it, as they both look at it.)

Do you want half?

FRAN: No I don't.

LEN: I'm only saying as a goodbye present, that's all. I'll keep it in me box. That's natural to have a thing like that anyway.

FRAN: I'm not saying it isn't.

LEN: Just let me put it away and forget about it now.

(Exits and re-enters.)

You'll buy 'em. Lucky bags and all that crap. With you, it'll be doll shit. Wait and see.

FRAN: Oh I'm ready me mate. I want it. Bring it on!

LEN: You know what I loved about me daughters? Back of their necks as girls. You don't see it in women, but the back of their necks all white and fluffy, and a bit of their jaw bone and cheek like a pillow, nose and eyelashes. Concentrating on something, and... thinking about the world in front of them. Beautiful. After a bit with your girls... they're always facing you. Maybe it's when they're sat on your knee. Winding them.

FRAN: Ha yeah, beautiful, until they do a big burp. You feel triumphant don't you?

LEN: Oh aye. Big burp for Daddy. Yeah. Ahhh. Yeah... that's it... when you don't make 'em burp or fart any more, you've lost them Franny. Gone.

FRAN: Me Mam used to say 'Don't talk to me like that, I used to wipe your arse!'

LEN: Did she balls. She couldn't wipe her own, never mind yours!

FRAN: I know! I'm making up for that though.

LEN: You was no better.

FRAN: I'm better now.

LEN: Well... you didn't have a clue.

FRAN: I didn't.

LEN: Not a clue.

FRAN: Yeah.

LEN: Mikey though, that's another story. He'd have learnt from our mistakes –

FRAN: We said didn't we –

LEN: There's more to your flesh and blood than what they are as a kid!

FRAN: I'm not doing it –

LEN: That's all I'm saying –

FRAN: I'll go now if you carry on –

LEN: What carries on –

FRAN: Memories –

LEN: You don't just exist in your childhood, do you? Look at you.

FRAN: We know that imagining what happened to him, it didn't help.

LEN: It did. It helped me.

FRAN: Well, you aren't hearing me so what's the point?

LEN: Your baby's an ugly bastard.

FRAN: You what?

LEN: But to you she'll be fucking gorgeous.

FRAN: You better apologise for that.

LEN: Alright, I'm sorry that all babies are ugly, it's not my fault. Beauty is in the eye of the beholder. I mean, take you for instance –

FRAN: Or you, you dog –

LEN: Hey I don't mean that, I mean like… a lot of people said to me at the time, 'Fran's a kid, what are you doing?'

FRAN: Leave it.

LEN: But I saw from my eyes in. That's what I saw, not what they said. About you using me for a mug –

FRAN: I'm not rising to it Len.

LEN: But when someone's out of the room or out of your life, that's all you've got isn't it? How is that any different from imagining what his life's like now?

FRAN: It's different.

LEN: How? Different from your baby pictures? How?

FRAN: Because my baby's around to see.

(Pause.)

I didn't mean it like that… I mean…

LEN: Yeah, but who really sees anything?

FRAN: I do! And me daughter! And me wife! I wake up in the morning, they're there, I touch them. They touch me, Len!

(Len is seemingly getting angry so Fran thinks about easing off. They become calmer.)

I'm not saying owt to be cruel.

LEN: Don't be silly. Just ignore me. It's my thing. She's got a yorkie. Pat from the Co-op.

FRAN: Fuckin' hell, you could lose that up your arse.

LEN: Thought I was a bit uncomfortable.

FRAN: Yeah, you farted before when a car passed.

LEN: Oh that must be it then, it don't like cars. When I need a shit, I'll take next door's cat up with me instead of the paper.

FRAN: You're funny, you.

LEN: It's not me love, it's life. I just put in the exclamation marks, that's all.

FRAN: Eh, get this – life with a baby is like being on crack –

LEN: Why say crack? What do you know about crack?

FRAN: I'm just going with the flow –

LEN: You're a dick'ead if you've gone down that road –

FRAN: Why would I do that –

LEN: Wasting what you've got on a bit of internal.

FRAN: You were talking about internal what you make from the inside of your eyes, what you on about?

LEN: You do that?

FRAN: No I don't do that! I was joking.

LEN: What a waste.

FRAN: I was joking with you!

LEN: You don't deserve your two feet if you do that, walking around the Earth when –

FRAN: I don't do that, you know I don't.

LEN: Breathing, living, walking around –

FRAN: Leave it now.

LEN: I can't believe it.

FRAN: Stop it now.

LEN: Well... I just hoped for the best with you. That you wouldn't take things for granted, I would hate that.

FRAN: I don't. And even if I did... it's... nothing to do with you. It's my life not yours... I'm grateful for everything you've done, and I'm alright. I've never done wrong to you to me or anyone since.

LEN: I've always looked out for you haven't I?

FRAN: Yes.

LEN: Helped you when I could? Got you bits of jobs... alright, nothing substantial but... bit of money here and there... I've made sure you were alright? Looked out for you, kept you safe –

FRAN: Yes.

LEN: I kept you safe.

FRAN: You did.

LEN: Always watching out for you.

FRAN: Why?

LEN: Why? Why? It's what you do, what any decent person would do.

FRAN: Why?

LEN: Why? For your sake, that's why, for you and your life.

FRAN: Why?

LEN: For fuck– why why why? What d'you want Franny? I'm not asking for a fucking medal!

FRAN: I just want you to say why you looked out for me, got me jobs got me round, talking about things and talking about Mikey.

LEN: Do we not remember him? And pay him his debt? Give him what he deserves? Is that wrong? Eh? To give a lad what he deserves?

FRAN: What do I deserve?

LEN: Well, I'd say... no, no... you've asked me, so I'll tell you what you deserve. You deserve to make the most out of the precious and lucky life you have. You deserve that. And I deserve –

FRAN: The truth, and to move on.

LEN: Oh. To move on. Do you know when I was a kid, I went to Scarborough for me holidays. Just once. That was the most wonderful time I had as a kid, and I still remember it. The best holiday hands down. What's going to happen now that's better or worse than what I've had?

FRAN: Nothing. You happy with what I've done then Len?

LEN: Yeah, you done a good job, here you are.

(Gives her some money.)

FRAN: Thanks mate. Much appreciated. I'm gonna spend this on gravel for the front garden.

LEN: Thanks mate, nice job, see you later.

FRAN: Shall I tell what is so great about my new baby?

LEN: No, you've said what you needed to say.

FRAN: Er... no... don't think so... you can listen to me now –

LEN: Night Fran.

FRAN: No. I'll tell you something. Since you've had me in a stranglehold all these years. You'll listen to something that's real. You should listen to my new story about my girl.

LEN: I've had you in a what?

FRAN: I don't owe you.

LEN: You ungrateful –.

FRAN: You fucking... don't make me say it.

LEN: I gave you a decent life.

FRAN: And you robbed me of being a child and nearly, very nearly an adult.

LEN: I gave you love. So don't be going down that route now. Cos if we go down that route –

FRAN: Go on Len – go there please go there, please –

LEN: I lost my son.

FRAN: So did I.

LEN: You should have woke up when you had him.

FRAN: I should have been at school.

LEN: You never went anyway.

FRAN: Because I was always with you.

LEN: You started it all.

FRAN: For a bit of love, yeah. And you knew that.

LEN: We lost him, because of you.

FRAN: He isn't lost! I was lost. He's not lost!

LEN: I've paid enough.

FRAN: No. You haven't. You have never in your life said sorry to me.

(Pause.)

LEN: *(Pouring drinks.)* Go on.

FRAN: Go on?

LEN: Tell me. About the baby. Just get it done with. Then you can go.

FRAN: We were gonna have lit candles but it was too hot. And this girl that won't even let me cough in case the neighbours hear, she made me open every door and window in the house as she fucking bellowed out to the world and the nurse and my being-born baby and how much she hated my guts. And she really did you know. When that baby was tearing her apart, she really hated me. But hatred and love in one is something I'm used to seeing Len, and so I drank it in because she had every right to hate me and ten minutes later, she loved me more than the world, and I felt the same. And we were responsible for a life. I smell her on me and I knew how you felt. With every thought about your son, every heart-wrenching minute without him and every fading memory before, and all you tried to do to make him present, through me. I know what you did. And I know how much you love the boy and the man that never was.

LEN: Remember, it was about ten years ago, when you were flagging the garden, we started talking about how he'd be a storyteller like me.

FRAN: But we don't know that, Len.

LEN: I think he would.

FRAN: No he wouldn't –

LEN: Why you saying that! Why you doing that to me! You said it.

FRAN: He might've done anything, good or bad.

LEN: It was you who said it, not me, when we were talking, just talking about how he would be.

FRAN: Because I felt like I took him from you. But I didn't. I was fifteen when I had him. And by the time I was twenty I had so much sorrow in my life you could have buried me. You didn't need to weigh me down with the responsibility.

LEN: What do you mean? I don't know what you mean...

FRAN: You try and... you try and make him Len but... it's not... well... it is real, but he's not here and we don't know.

LEN: I don't know what you're talking about Fran! You're not making sense.

FRAN: Alright, it doesn't matter, let's forget... NO, no it's not fair that, I've done this all these... I've done it a long time... and you should know that I've done it for you...

LEN: What are you talking about Fran! Done what!? Eh!? Are you on about the jobs? Because I've paid you, haven't I?

FRAN: I'm not on about the jobs

LEN: I've got a lot of nothing!

FRAN: It's so... it's so sad Len...

LEN: If it makes me happy...

FRAN: It doesn't make you happy Len, it hasn't worked and it is never gonna work mate, it's just making something from nothing. And it doesn't make me happy at all.

LEN: It's a little bit out of your time.

FRAN: I've paid enough. And so have you.

LEN: Don't talk crap.

FRAN: I'm going now Len.

LEN: Please. Just do it. Just tell me. One more time. And I'll record it on me phone. I'll never ask you again. Never.

FRAN: We have a son called Mikey who lives round the corner from us. He did move away to study but is very much a home bird. He's got your brains and so he went to Uni to study like you always should have done. He travelled for a year after Uni, he went to a lot of the places you wanted to go when you were younger. People always used to think that you were his older brother when you first went out drinking with him. He is healthy and athletic and goes running a lot, he never wanted to take drugs and hang about with the lads round here, but he doesn't mind you having a drink. He was always good at writing stories and poems, but he was a hard lad so no one took the piss out of him. He helps anyone out in need or in trouble, he's a good young man and a good laugh, has a great sense of humour. He's... very handsome, he looks a lot like you did when you were his age. He loves his family and sees them a lot. You're close and he always says you'll be his best man one day. You've never had a bad word for each other, in all these years. I was a very young when I had him and was a crap mum, but you were bringing up two young daughters half of the week who you adored and so were a really good Dad by the time Mikey came around. When Mikey was five he was in a paddling pool in our front garden playing with a beach ball. His sisters had a tea set and were having a pretend picnic on the grass. I had just nipped out to get some more cans from Papa's off licence round the corner. Mikey's beach ball blew over the hedge and onto the road, he ran to the get it out of the garden, but just before he got to the road you were pulling up in the car and he saw you. And it's a good job, because you went right over the beach ball. That could have been Mikey. But it wasn't. And we've always thought that popping the beach ball made him think carefully about roads and be a responsible person. And that is the whole story. Of our son. Michael.

(As Fran approaches Len the lights slowly brighten and 'What Becomes of the Broken Hearted' by Jimmy Ruffin plays loudly enough for the audience to make any noise they wish and it won't be heard.)

(Fran stands over Len and holds his shoulders, kisses him on the head and slowly lifts it without any embarrassment. She leans down then and looks at him, embraces him, then leaves.)

(This should lead in to the verse "The roots of love grow all around..." and the lights then slowly fade.)

THE DEMON DOG OF WATERHEAD

"Sharp and very funny."
David Cunningham, British Theatre Guide

"Touching ... with a deeper message."
Jack Wagman, Number 9

Premiered at Hope Mill Theatre, Manchester, 2022

The Demon Dog of Waterhead portraits a couple forced to re-evaluate their marriage and their success as parents following the loss of their dog, Jimmy Mac.

CAST (5)

SUE

A woman in her early 50s. Sue has her own business in vintage stuff. She loves live events, especially music festivals, but stopped going to Glastonbury when you could no longer sneak under the fence, and now prefers the small, secret, niche festivals. Sue works hard and is very sociable, generous, and has a lot of girlfriends. She takes great pictures and that's part of why her business is so successful. She used to be a hairdresser, but a back injury changed her lifestyle a lot. She is troubled by all the injustice of the world, and by Dom consistently changing his opinions. In lockdown, when they spent a lot of time together, she had to order some baby spoons so that she didn't have to hear Dom stirring his tea, making a *ding-a-ling* noise. Sue listens properly to people; it's taken her many years, but she does pride herself on that. She tries to walk in other people's shoes because, growing up in a problematic home and having a child at a young age, she was forever having to explain herself and fight to be heard and seen. When Dawn needed help due to health problems as a baby and a young child, Sue had to become a responsible adult very quickly. And so, when she has the chance, she loves to let herself go. She has become fearful of Dom dying and doesn't hide it very well.

DOM

In his early 60s, a hospital porter who is also in a folk band, and Sue's partner. Dom and Sue split up when their daughter Dawn was a baby. He then tried to be a playboy heartbreaker, it was not a good look for him and he couldn't carry it off, especially pushing around the pram. It was a sad time in his life, but within a year he got his act together in one of his many forthcoming attempts to be the man he that he feels Sue deserves. He is at his funniest when he is frustrated or angry, which riles him even more as he knows Sue will be laughing – although that's now, not when they were younger, when his temper and hangovers were a real problem. Dom is always going to be a joyous and emotional 12-year-old lad. He is an ideas person who's had many hobbies, and reads all the time. If he reads a self-help book, he'll be bound by that philosophy for at least a month and then forget to be. If he reads a great novel, he becomes influenced by the lead character's life for a while too. He is always passing on things he's learnt to the glassy-eyed attention of his mates. He tries not to drink anymore, but sometimes still gets leathered.

NICKY
Sue and Dom's friend, a gay Mancunian man in his 50s.

MANDY
A friend.

ANN
A friend.

SCENE 1: JIMMY IS THROWN A BALL

Low, dramatic lights on stage.

Sue is spotlit in deep thought, staring out across the audience. She is wearing a large brown jumper that engulfs her and yet holds herself as if she is cold.

>**SUE:** All that there is, is this one time, one ticket for life and then silence. Absolutely endless voids of nothingness. Life just ebbs away.

(A figure is seen to enter – it is Dom – who watches Sue from the silhouette of a doorway, before slowly approaching her.)

>We must carry on. We must endure.

>*Dom stands on a squeaky toy and lights flash up. He is wearing a brown t-shirt and pants and has hound dog ears on.*

>**DOM:** Told you not to have a drink last night. I'm not listening to this crap all fucking day. Get a Berocca!

(He potters about.)

>**SUE:** I'm not hungover Dom, I'm grieving. And still drunk.

>**DOM:** I can't sort it all out while you look out the window crying all morning. Sue –

>**SUE:** What's the point? Everyone hated him.

>**DOM:** Sue –

>**SUE:** Bet everyone's glad he's dead.

>**DOM:** Sue... Nicky, Mandy and Ann are coming at eleven.

>**SUE:** So?

>**DOM:** Sue –

>**SUE:** I'm too sad for this. I don't want to be fun, I want to curl up on his bed and sleep for a month.

>**DOM:** Look, the ashes have arrived...

(Dom produces a giant firework rocket with 'Jimmy Mac' written on the side.)

>**SUE:** So?

>**DOM:** Sue –

>**SUE:** Shut up Dom, stop saying 'Sue' every two seconds. I'm just very very very very sad.

>**DOM:** You'll feel better when you're in your onesie.

SUE: No one ever feels better in a onesie, Dom. All people feel in a onesie is defeat.

(Hugs the firework.)

What you gonna say about the firework?

DOM: I'm gonna say 'It's not like he ever wanted to fly, we just needed his DNA to be as far away from the house as possible.'

SUE: I've saved some of the ashes for Dawn.

DOM: She's not coming today.

SUE: You don't have to keep reminding me she didn't want to come. But she will eventually visit and the dog will still be dead.

DOM: And mostly shot up into the air.

SUE: Yes and the rest of him in a tupperware box for our daughter. Because I'm kind.

DOM: And what do you think she's going to do with them?

SUE: Shove them up her arse, I don't care.

(Sue brings in and inspects the trays of food.)

Open the buck's fizz Dom, will you?

DOM: You're not having a drink today; I'm not dealing with that.

SUE: Alright, don't shit yourself, it's non-alcoholic.

DOM: Right, good job.

SUE: Carry on dictating though, and I will have a drink Dom.

(Sue runs off up the stairs.)

It's my choice not yours! I'll have a ton of it if I want!

DOM: *(Shouting after her.)* Do that and you'll be sleeping in the bath, you're not pissing on the mattress two nights running! Hi Nicky, hi Mandy.

(Nicky and Mandy have entered wearing furry onesies and with their faces painted like dogs. Dom hugs them.)

Thanks for dressing up, Nicky.

MANDY: No problem. Keeps our clothes free from the hair. *(Sniffs up.)* His spirit lives on...

DOM: Maybe don't say that to Sue, Mandy. She's a little bit upset today.

NICKY: It is very much as if he's still here though, Dom.

MANDY: In many ways, yes. Have you hoovered since his passing?

DOM: We can't get rid of it all! They keep emerging out of nowhere.

(Dom puts a giant picture of a dog onto an easel – it's hard to make out what kind, we just see jaws, slaver, and tongue, but they've done it in black and white to make it look 'artsy'.)

(Dom lights candles around the picture.)

NICKY: Well, my left leg can tell you he's not here, that's for sure.

DOM: We did keep saying Nicky, don't wear white jeans.

NICKY: I'm a traditional gay Mancunian in his fifties, Dom. I only have white jeans. Hi Ann, are you not on the WhatsApp group?

(Ann enters dressed as a cat.)

ANN: What do you mean?

(Dom gets a text.)

DOM: Oh right... here we go... Alexa? Play Jimmy Mac.

SCENE 2: JIMMY SHOOTS OFF

As the song plays, Sue enters on all fours, in a onesie and hound ears, lip-synching to 'Jimmy Mac'. She does a dance, begging into death drop, tail wagging, scrapping with and chasing Ann.

SUE: Nicky and Mandy and Ann. We have invited you here today to celebrate the life of our beloved dog Jimmy Mac.

ANN: What's that?!

(Ann has moved a cushion as she sat down and it seems has sat in the late Jimmy Mac's slaver.)

DOM: Sorry Ann, it's his ecto-slaver we think, it keeps appearing. I'll get you a wet-wipe. There you go – now feel free to tuck in, we've all his favourite food – wotsits, crusts and flumps. Bucks fizz for anyone?

SUE: Right...

(When everyone is settled, Sue bangs a microphone that has been fashioned into a bone and stands on a pouffe reading from a note.)

When our daughter Dawn decided to selfishly embark on a life of her own, we thought we would replace her with something more grateful – a rescue dog. On our way to Manchester Dog's Home, me and Dom talked about how nice it would be – country walks, throwing a stick, having a pint in The Swan by the fire – with an adorable little fella curled at our feet. But on that day the choices were either staffies, which Dom's scared of...

DOM: It's just that they remind me of the demons from Ghostbusters.

SUE: ...knackered old terriers, or the legendary repeat inmate and long-time veteran of the kennels – Jimmy Mac. The card on his kennel said 'We tried to get him done but the vet refused after damn near losing his own testicles trying to anaesthetise him. Be warned, he's randy.' And it said that everyone loved him... And that it was going to take a particular kind of owner to give him a forever home – and when we saw him – massive, matted, facing the back of his cell, giving us the side-eye, we knew that we were that particular kind of owner – bereft, needy and very, very stoned. For ten long years we put up with him. His barking, his destructiveness, his slime. He had a faux fur look about him and felt like an old carpet that was dumped in a field over winter. No amount of baths and potions could take away the smell of stilton and sprouts. But you know, perfect is boring. And for all that, he had the best cuddles in the world. He was a nightmare yes, but he was our nightmare. To Jimmy!

(They all cheer. Nicky, Mandy and Ann think that's all they have to endure.)

And now begins the slide show – Dom – LIGHTS PLEASE!

(Dom turns the lights out and is lit in a spotlight with a guitar facing the slideshow which is happening on the 4th-wall and is represented by flickering lights across their faces. Sue sits watching the slides with love.)

(As the other three face the audience and flickers of light shine on them they react to slides of ten years of Jimmy, sympathetically at first, then glazing over, and then by mid-way into the song they are all in slide show hell.)

DOM: *(Sings.)*

'There's a hole in our heart and it can't be healed
By a dog that can heal
No sappy cockapoo
Can replace his runny doggy do
Or
Chew up my most expensive shoe
There's only you
Jimmy Mac
The dog that got me the sack
And irreparably damaged Susan's back

(Unseen by the others, Nicky gets up, stretches his legs, and goes upstage to the portrait of Jimmy and the rocket with Jimmy's ashes, where he laughs fondly and reads the inscription on the it.)

(The crepe tassels at the bottom of the rocket are very close to the candles...)

> So keep your clever collies
> Your shiny spaniels and your labs
> We will miss his eye infections
> And his weeping belly scabs
> He cost us five years' holidays
> On fungal infections and bowel disease
> And not forgetting his immortal fleas

(Nicky accidentally lights the rocket and is in peril, moving this way and that until he runs offstage and we see a flash of light.)

> No sappy cockapoo
> Can replace his runny doggy-do
> Or
> Chew up my most expensive shoe
> There's only you
> Jimmy Mac
> Only you

(Nicky returns unseen, covered in ash and with his hair on end, carrying what's left of the rocket.)

> There's only you
> Jimmy Mac
> Only you'

(Mandy and Ann are shunted out of their almost slumber and begin to clap as Dom puts the lights on.)

(Everyone turns to look at Nicky who is covered in Jimmy's ashes.)

NICKY: I'm okay. Don't worry.

SUE: Well, I guess he couldn't bear to be apart from you, Nicky.

(Sue slumps.)

(Dom lets everyone out in a flurry of sympathy and apologies.)

SCENE 3: JIMMY FETCHES

Dom takes off his ears, then Sue's ears, and sits down to look at the slideshow which is replaying.

SUE: I wonder why our Dawn didn't want to come.

DOM: It's not her scene is it? All our mates and dog outfits.

SUE: She loved him though, she thought he was as daft as us.

DOM: As thick as us, she said.

SUE: Yeah. She loves us but... she doesn't think we were the world's best parents does she? We weren't rubbish – just a bit messy.

DOM: We did what we could with our resources.

SUE: But still – I would like the time again. Wouldn't you?

DOM: Yeah, to be able to like, hold her hand and that.

SUE: And blow raspberries on her belly?

DOM: Yeah... aww... I wish for the time again sometimes, redo it you know –

SUE: Yeah. You were a bit of a dick.

DOM: Don't, Sue. You're not without fault.

SUE: Is it difficult to love me?

DOM: Is it balls. We've both had our moments. And to be fair, she's thirty now and about to have a baby. Think she's moved on.

SUE: Yeah but, she's my baby, that's not changed.

DOM: She'll remember us fondly.

SUE: What do you mean by that Dom? She'll remember us fondly?

DOM: You know, when we've gone.

SUE: Why are you saying that? Is something wrong with you?

DOM: No!

SUE: Don't you dare die before I learn to drive, Dom!

DOM: We're going round tomorrow don't forget, I'm putting the cot up for her.

SUE: We might not be great at the admin, but our manual labour skills are second to none. And of course, you're no one if you haven't been let down by your Mum and Dad. We took her everywhere, didn't we?

DOM: Yeah, she's got nice memories. Remember the pedalos in Barca?

SUE: You're always going on about the pedalos in Barca, Dom, like we never did anything good but the pedalos in Barca. What about the fire eating at The Green Man? What about kite making at Kendal Calling? What about the paragliding in Turkey?

DOM: I would keep that paragliding quiet, she was five, it was probably neglect.

SUE: Hmmm. She loved it though. I don't think kids realise that you want them to be proud of you too. And another thing people don't realise – there isn't a separate compartment for the love you have for your dog. It's all one love. Keep wanting to whistle, like he's in the kitchen.

DOM: It's hard. Gonna be hard for a while.

SUE: We've done what we could to be good and caring to an utter arsehole. Like we will with the baby, even if that's an arsehole.

(There is a knock at the door. No one reacts for a moment.)

DOM: I'll go then, shall I?!

SUE: Yes, you will go. CAN YOU NOT SEE I'M UPSET!

(Dom exits then returns carrying a box with something moving within. He brings it forward and they both peer inside then jump. Dom quickly puts the box down. Sue tears off a note from the side of the box and they both back away from it.)

SUE: *(Reads.)* 'We thought our prize-winning dog was expecting cockerpoos from a kennel club endorsed stud we introduced to her a few months ago. Fortunately for you, we have got away with selling most of them, except for this one. This one is unmistakeably like that thing of yours. It's up to you, you can either take this runt off our hands or you can bring him back and reimburse us for the vet bills for all ten of the puppies your mutt has clearly fathered. Anita, 25 Green Street. P.S. Sorry for your loss. P.P.S. Fix that fence. P.P.P.S. He will only eat wotsits.'

(Facing upstage, they walk towards the box, look down at it, look at each other, back at the box and put their arms round each other's backs.)

Premiered at greenroom, Manchester, 2005

A breastfeeding class for pregnant mothers is led by an interesting character.

"She epitomises the decline of the NHS and is an example of the 'double-glazing salesmen' way in which they are determined that you make your offspring chomp at your nipples until you fear and hate your beautiful baby to its very cutesy-pie core." *CC*

CAST (1)

MELODY COFFEY

The breastfeeding advisor at a hospital, and for whom life would have no purpose without the concept of breastfeeding.

SCENE 1

MELODY: Hiya, my name's Melody Coffey and I'm the breastfeeding advisor for the hospital. I've been running these sessions for a couple of years now, making mums aware of the benefits of the breast, and I have recently been awarded a certificate from the Breastfeeding Council of Great Britain for my work in this field.

First of all, let me give you a bit of background. There is nothing more natural and rewarding than feeding your new-born baby. It makes sure your baby receives all the nutrients it needs for its tiny little body to be nurtured as nature intended. Now, some people are going to find it very difficult and others will be squirting like nobody's business, but the important thing is not to give up.

Right ladies, as you might have guessed we're now going to talk about latching on. So, I've given out me plastic babies, hope you've all got one. And I hope you've got the right colour baby. If not, swap them around.

If you have a look under your chairs you'll see I've placed a pair of comedy knockers. I collected these from my colleague Fiona's hen party in Palma as I think they're a cracking tool to save Mum's embarrassment, so if you can slip them over your head by the elastic – smashing.

Okay, now cradle your new-born and get into a comfortable position. You use your thumb and index finger to erect your nipple, it could take a bit of time, I don't know, it depends on you.

Now what you do is take your hard nipple and gently stroke your new-born baby on the cheek, until it eventually turns its head towards you. Now, the first time I tried to get my baby to latch on was in the delivery room and I was having my stitches done and the epidural had worn off and the last thing I wanted to do was to stroke my nipple across somebody's face, but if I can do it in that horrific circumstance anyone can, let me tell you.

So our new-born has turned towards our breast. Don't just shove your nipple in its mouth as it might find this very disturbing. Just, you know, allow the baby to do all the work. But remember the new-born has to have the whole lot in because sucking on the end won't produce milk just painful bruising and cracked and bleeding tissue. Now watch my face, when your baby is doing this...

(Does rhythmical sucking.)

...that's when they are receiving your nutritious colostrums, leading up to your period of engorgement when your breasts will become very sore, hard and swollen. And you will, I know it seems mad, but you will love this happening because it will mean your milk's there.

Now that's all we're going to cover of the logistics for today because I want to get on with your questions. So in case anyone turned up a bit late, I asked you to write on me little post-its any queries you might have about feeding your little new-borns and fathers too, or even friends or family, that's fine. So I've collected them all in, here we go...

(Reads.) 'Is breastfeeding painful?'

(Thinks about this.)

It can be, but this is almost always overridden by the special closeness and nurturing of it all. One Mum described it as 'the very essence of my soul being sucked away by Satan' but others just say it's lovely, so...

Erm...

(Reads.) 'My mother tried to breastfeed me but wasn't producing enough milk. She was left to do it until a midwife at home advised her that I was starving and to give me... (With disgust.) ...formula.'

Has your Mum got small nipples? Is she here? Well we won't know if I'm right then will we, but I would say it's probably a case of you not sucking on your Mum properly because she hadn't got her nipples hard enough. Anyway, bring her next week and I'll get you latched on. As I said, don't give up!

Okay, just one more – here we are...

(Reads.) 'I have not yet decided whether to breastfeed because this question is niggling me: is breast feeding oppressive to women? It does seem very controlling and quite torturous, also, it makes sure the woman is unable to have any kind of freedom away from the child, would you say this is a possible theory as to why the powers that be our so keen on women to breastfeed?'

(Thinks.)

No.

Okay then, next session amongst other subjects we will be covering breastfeeding twins and clogged milk ducts. I'll see you next week then. Can you please before you go, can you please give me comedy knockers a wipe down, because some of you will be slightly lactating by now and it's not very nice for the next class that.

Bye everyone.

FIVE WOMEN: RAMBLING

"Pitch perfect." Peter Ruddick, North West End

"A subtleness and lightness of touch which puts it in a different class." David Chadderton, British Theatre Guide

Premiered at 53two, Manchester, 2022

Five retired nurses in their seventies go for an overnight adventure, each now at a changing point in their lives.

"*Five Women: Rambling* explores lifelong female friendships, their depth, support and strength. It looks at the changes life brings us, whilst wrapped in the support of those around us, and how we really only age on the outside." CC

CAST (6)

LINDA

As a young girl, Linda was all bike rides and cartwheels. She played out every day, even in the rain. She could never keep clean, always climbing trees, making dens, building ramps, but then one day everyone decided to grow up. So she had to slow down and pretend she had too. And she's been doing that ever since. But now she is going back to the person she was aged 8 and it feels wonderful, even though others are a little fearful of it. Linda married young, but her husband died and she brought up her three children on her own through their teenage years. One of them has a child now, and having a grandchild has been like all her Christmases came at once. She is enjoying the new look of the world and forgetting a lot.

JENNY

Jenny is tired of a lot of things now, mainly centred around what she has learnt about the flaws and shortcomings of others. She is angry about life and everywhere she turns the narrative is plain to her: people are arseholes and let you down. It's exhausting being this furious, so she spends her downtime swimming (people better move out of her way and not chat in the baths!), gardening, and singing show tunes in the back bedroom, dressed-up, into the mirror. All this is great, but she has become lonely. She has upset Sandra and misses her friendship. She knows she expected too much of her and that she has kicked back, and wishes that things could go back to how they were. Jenny is dry, flamboyant, and she is mostly right. For some reason that she never gets, everyone loves her.

ANNE

Anne has cultivated this group; she is the quiet leader. She knows she's nice, knows she does nice things, and is very giving. She's tried very hard to get to this stage, to have grace and compassion, but something fierce sleeps in her heart and it occasionally awakens – and it knows no fear. Growing up, Anne experienced some horrors in her life, then with several partners who preyed on her (at the time) vulnerability. It's for this reason she wanted to go into caring for people and helping them recover physically and mentally. She is spending this time in quiet reflection of her life because something is going to change and limit its future, and it now feels that it is time to take stock. She will tend to her friends and she will enjoy their love back, and she will be grateful for the gift of them. She has gravitas.

JOSIE

Josie has been around the block, she's partied most of her life – no one ever knew how she managed to do a full shift, but she was born with a wick at both ends. She has anecdotes and philosophical throw-away moments. People tell her what she has said to them in the past, things that stuck with them for life, and she remembers none of it. She's a beacon in the LGBTQ+ community; a trailblazer and a survivor of the coal face who lifts others. But when she crashes no one can get into the cave her thoughts have forced her into.

SANDRA

Sandra is hugely intelligent. Like, genius intelligent. It's not a big deal for her to work things out that others never can. She qualified as a surgeon but didn't like the distance between her and the patients, so retrained and was the intensive care sister. She was more than that – everyone called on her, becoming a guardian angel to new doctors. Sandra can't quieten her mind. She has an allotment, is the archivist for the local museum, is a mentor for single older people who are terminally ill, and is on several boards. She's very direct, as she feels that's the right way to be, and can offend the easily offended. Sandra likes things her way and can be frustrated if they don't go as she planned. She has felt very free since a fall out with Jenny has given her much needed time alone. Rules need to be in place for the future she feels, or Jenny will never let her alone. When something can't be done and she hears "Give it to Sandra", she always feels pride. She can sometimes feel like a hero.

GREEN WOMAN

Always unseen by the cast, she represents Mother Earth/Green Man folklore.

SCENE 1: ARRIVAL

Green Woman enters with a guitar.

> **GREEN WOMAN:** *(Sings.)*
> 'Are old friends a lasting reflection
> of things that are said and done?
> When friends are together
> is the past really ever a time that's gone?
> Up on the hills away from their lives
> are they mother's, sisters, carers and wives?
> Or just old friends?'

The women enter in a whirlwind. Talking over each other, rambling, excited. There is no real let up to this so audience will have a journey of relentless rambling.

> **LINDA:** Oh it's lovely. This was a good choice.
>
> **JOSIE:** Here we are!
>
> **ANNE:** Here she is! Aww, hello sweetheart!
>
> **JOSIE:** Oh you look lovely with your hair that colour –
>
> **ANNE:** Put your bag inside –
>
> **SANDRA:** Right, right, yes, yes, okay yes. Hello love! You look lovely! Your hair's so lovely that colour.
>
> **JOSIE:** I need some advice later – sunken patios –
>
> **SANDRA:** Don't you get me leathered again.
>
> **LINDA:** Hi!
>
> **SANDRA:** Hiya. I hope you've grown up since last time –
>
> **LINDA:** Oh doesn't it feel differently already in this air? I bet this is going to be the best get together ever, don't you?
>
> **JOSIE:** I thought you might have a way of doing it, you know?
>
> **SANDRA:** I just need to get this phone on charge –
>
> **JOSIE:** What we don't want is some dickhead messing it up – mainly me!
>
> **JENNY:** I'm not meant to carry things like that. Why is there not room for more than two cars? Do you know what the situation is with that car park?

JOSIE: Eh, stop moaning, we're meant to be on a jolly, sit down and take the weight off your crocs –

SANDRA: How are you sweetheart? I just need to put this phone on charge –

LINDA: I haven't really brought much. I've got a picnic set I got for me and Poppy. I'll bring that in.

JENNY: Oh I'm fine, ignore me.

ANNE: We've all got a windows. Josie you've dropped your glasses –

LINDA: I've brought the Factor 50 –

ANNE: Ah, there's ma darlin'.

LINDA: It's what me and Poppy use, Factor 50.

JENNY: What they wanna do is flatten all these hills and make a bigger car park. They're me gardening croc but they're good for walking in, people don't realise.

LINDA: Hey, do you fancy walking to the top res later? It's meant to be gorgeous there.

JENNY: I would have been here sooner but I was behind a tractor from Huddersfield Road to Delph – some teenager on a mobile. Hey, I need to be near a window or I'll feel like I'm suffocating –

ANNE: We've all got a windows!

JOSIE: We've all got a windows!

ANNE: And I don't mind where anyone wants to go, but the two bedroom one is me and Linda, I hope she doesn't mind. Sandra?! There's a complex air con system that needs sorting, or it'll be retired nurses roasting in their own juices.

SANDRA: Right, I've sorted the air con, just no one touch it now. Right. Lunch. I've got a load of green beans off the allotment; we can barbeque them or something.

ANNE: In the fridge there are some egg sandwiches already made up, courtesy of your chickens Sandra.

SANDRA: I love egg!

JENNY: I love egg!

LINDA: I love egg as well!

ANNE: And some wine, and beers chilling for later cos we're having a barbeque!

JENNY: Do you know what the situation is with the car park? Is it free after six?

ANNE: Jenny, I'm going to move my car to a space that's two huts down, I've asked a nice couple if I can park there –

LINDA: Oh, I'm definitely bringing Poppy up here. Are we going swimming? If we're going swimming, can somebody do me a French plait please?

JOSIE: Has anybody got a first aid kit? I've caught me hand on that gate! Anyone? Load of retired ICU nurses and no one's got a fucking plaster!

SANDRA: There's a first aid kit in the kitchen.

LINDA: Oh I'm loving this feeling of freedom!

JENNY: Arseholes on the road, every one of them. Apart from me.

SCENE 2: LUNCH

They have stopped, a little exhausted, at an idyllic spot for lunch and are all squashed up on one rock. It's tense, intense and awkward.

Jenny gives out a box of sandwiches and markedly misses out Sandra, who gets her own without any fuss.

JENNY: Flies.

(Pause with the occasional sigh at the beauty of the place. There is lots of flasks and chewing, With Jenny exaggerating the fly situation.)

LINDA: *(To Anne.)* I'm definitely bringing my granddaughter Poppy here; she'll love this stream.

JENNY: As the midges do.

SANDRA: That's the thing about the country –

JENNY: I think I'm ready to move on in a minute.

SANDRA: Buzzing with nature – everywhere you go –

JENNY: There's less flies a bit further back from the stream.

JOSIE: *(To Anne.)* This is line dancing all over again.

SANDRA: Come on then Jenny, let's go to the flyless area of the country – just up the path.

JENNY: Are you okay Sandra?

SANDRA: Why wouldn't I be okay?

JENNY: It's just you seem a little bit put out –

SANDRA: I'm fine –

JENNY: Well, that's good then, sometimes other people have better judgment than you that's all –

SANDRA: Come on everyone, Jenny's got a problem so we need to be at her beckoned call –

JOSIE: Here it comes –

JENNY: No… no, it's you that's got the problem love, you cut people off, just like that. *(Clicks fingers.)*

SANDRA: People, have lives –

JENNY: Just like that. *(Clicks fingers.)*

SANDRA: No.

('Just like that' finger-clicks and 'No' goes on and on with no way of anyone knowing or caring what the argument is about.)

(Linda collects leaves and stones whilst Josie and Anne pack up.)

SANDRA: I am not going there with you ever again. And that is the end of it.

JENNY: You can't do anything that's out of your comfort zone. And now I've nothing to do. Nothing at all.

JOSIE: What is it? I'll come with you Jenny!

JENNY: We were going to trampolinercise –

JOSIE: I'm not doing that.

JENNY: And Sandra's took a dislike to the instructor as she always does.

SANDRA: It's a cult.

JENNY: It's not a cult just because he's enigmatic –

SANDRA: It's a cult –

LINDA: Oh I might get my Poppy a trampoline, she's so fun you know –

JENNY: I love bouncing! And you've ripped that trampoline from under me.

LINDA: Oh that's not on Sandra, she could have got hurt!

JOSIE: Don't be giving him any money Jenny. I mean, apart from for the trampolining.

JENNY: Every time we join something you say they're looking at us funny, or it's a pyramid scheme or a cult –

SANDRA: And every time it is what I say –

(Green Women enters.)

GREEN WOMAN: *(Sings.)*

'In winter she's brittle and cold,
then spring picks the scabs off her limbs.
In summer she's luscious and bold,
then autumn she's wrinkled and letting things go.'

SCENE 3: SWIMMING

Anne is sat on her own with all the bags around her. She has a little pad out and has inks and paints.

We can hear noises at a huge distance – splashing, screaming; the others having a great time.

Anne paints them in the water.

The actors should be right at the back of audience to give a good distance, so that if Anne speaks at a normal level we hear every word, but if they yell, it is still slightly quieter than Anne, and they can't hear her.

SANDRA: Are you going to get in Josie?

JOSIE: I'm parading first.

JENNY: Just get in you soft-arse!

JOSIE: You know you're not supposed to swim in a reservoir.

LINDA: It's okay Josie, we're miles away from the plughole here.

JENNY: There's nothing to be scared of.

ANNE: Apart from the pikes!

SANDRA: Are you watching us Anne?

ANNE: *(Waves and nods.)* Daft old bats.

JOSIE: One, two, threeeeeeeeeeee!

(Josie dive bombs in. Lots of screaming and noises of being freezing.)

(Anne gets up and watches for a moment, concerned.)

JENNY: That's how people drown you prick!

JOSIE: Whooohoooooo!

(Anne checks her watch and has some tablets. She listens to them and watches them. Her eyes tear up.)

SANDRA: This is the life!

JENNY: Oh yeah, freedom.

JOSIE: Look at us all back together again.

SANDRA: Hey, we'll get Anne in next time.

JENNY: Yeah! Let's come back here next year and make Anne get in with us. What's up Josie?

JOSIE: Nothing.

ANNE: Don't tell them Josie. Not now.

(Anne looks at her little water colour and is pleased. She leaves it to dry. She then takes out five little gift bags and puts them in each of the other's bags. They are heard laughing and messing around in the water. Anne is content.)

SANDRA: Oi! Are you gonna get in next year Anne?!

ANNE: Next year...

(Anne takes her trousers and top off and heads towards the water.)

(From the distance.) There might not be a next yeaaaaaaaaaaar it'sssss fuckiiiiiing freeeezing!

(Green Woman enters.)

GREEN WOMAN: *(Sings.)*
'She waves on
welcoming breezes.
She stays on
like the life of a tree.
Like poetry.'

SCENE 4: SUPPER

The sun's gone down. There are remnants of supper and wine, and cushions and solar lights are out.

They all have dayglo headbands or necklaces on.

They have a sheet pulled tight and are in the middle of bouncing Jenny high in the air as the lights come up.

ALL: Waaaaay! Waaaay! Waaaay!

(They lower her. Jenny is giggling more than anyone has in their life.)

SANDRA: Right, now shut up about the trampolining.

LINDA: Remember when we used to do that on the ICU?!

JENNY: We didn't Sandra. *(Mouths 'Shut it' to Linda.)*

SANDRA: You better not have done!

JOSIE: We never did that, sister. Only if they were in a coma.

(Linda runs off laughing to get a nice cushion to sit on and is out of earshot.)

JENNY: *(Aside, to Sandra)* What's Linda on?

SANDRA: It's being around a kid I think, it's rubbing off on her.

(Anne chilly and puts the bedsheet round herself. Everyone thanks her for the glowing necklaces.)

JOSIE: *(Aside to Anne.)* Are you okay?

ANNE: I'm happy and really enjoying all this, being in the moment.

JOSIE: Don't let me forget to get a nice stone for Louise. She loves all that kind of shit.

JENNY: Is there such a thing as a nice stone?

JOSIE: Oh yeah. She has a load of them in a bowl. It's her thing.

SANDRA: Remember how Josie said that she would never be with the one person when there was so many women in the world? Now she has a wife with a stone bowl.

JENNY: Yeah, and she does nothing for herself now. Went to pick her up the other day, Lou was tying her laces.

JOSIE: I had a bad back!

SANDRA: She does all the meals as well, Anne told me.

ANNE: Here you go, you can have this one.

JOSIE: Where've you got that from?

ANNE: The driveway.

JOSIE: You're all just jealous because I hit the jackpot.

LINDA: I feel like I hit the jackpot with my little Poppy. The light that shines through her eyes is golden, it's more beautiful than any gem I've ever seen in my life.

JOSIE: Who's Poppy, Linda? I've never heard you talk about her? … Hey, I'm only messing.

LINDA: It's okay, I know I never shut up about her, it's just such a nice thing she came along. I'm sure it'll all get ruined in time.

ANNE: Oh Linda, don't say that, it'll be wonderful.

JENNY: Well, she's right, there's always a shit side.

LINDA: HAHAHAHAHAHAHAHAH Jenny, there is, there is! You've just made me remember – I got off with this lad the night before my graduation I'd always fancied. We had a great night, I put my fingers up his bottom. Then in the morning my Mum and Dad met me for the ceremony, they were so proud of me. My graduation picture sat proudly in their front window for everyone to see. That girl in the picture, who didn't know she'd spend years living hand to mouth, bringing up kids on her own. That girl in the picture, only I could tell, but if you looked close enough, you could see on the hand holding the scroll, there's a bit of poo under each cuticle. There's always a shit side.

(This story hangs in the air.)

JENNY: *(To Sandra.)* I hope I remember that in the morning.

SANDRA: That was a corker.

ANNE: *(To Josie.)* I'm not following that. You coming in Linda?

(They all take their glowing jewellery off and go in apart from Linda.)

LINDA: Do I have to?

JENNY: No Linda you can do what you like, g'night –

(Jenny, Sandra and Anne go in, leaving their glowing necklaces.)

LINDA: Do you want to have a cry Josie?

JOSIE: What? No I... what? Where's that come from?

LINDA: It's okay, I know you're sad about Anne. It's good to have a good cry, you don't always have to be the brave one.

JOSIE: How do you she's...? I'm not... ...I'm fine. It's just, she's going to be in pain and suffer. It's not fair.

LINDA: No

JOSIE: And... is it worth being with like, at this stage in me life, like, Louise, if one of us is going to die? Before Louise, I'd only ever really loved Anne. This is daft this, but... Have I jinxed Anne?

LINDA: Don't be silly. You don't have superpowers Josie. You're not that important.

JOSIE: Thanks Linda. Why can't we get better and younger as we get wiser?

LINDA: It is sad that everything changes. But we have to make room don't we, for the next lot?

(Josie cries and Linda comforts her. Linda gives her a stone.)

I was going to give it Poppy, but I want you to have it.

(Josie gives Linda a kiss, takes the stone and exits.)

(As the light fades completely, Linda is in darkness playing with the glowing jewellery.)

SCENE 5: LEAVING

Bags are coming out.

Sandra and Jenny talk over each other. Josie and Anne are rambling too, but seem worked up.

      JOSIE: *(To Sandra and Jenny.)* Heads up, Linda didn't go to bed –

(Linda appears from nowhere still with the necklaces on. She holds a buttercup.)

      LINDA: Let's see who likes butter. Do you like butter Josie? Oh yes, Josie likes butter. Do you like butter Jenny? Yes, Jenny likes butter. What about you Anne? Oh, Anne doesn't like butter. What about Sandra? Sandra does – do me now Sandra? Sandra? Do I like butter?

(Sandra, alarmed, checks if Linda likes butter.)

(Pause.)

(There's a confirmation now from everyone that Linda has changed slightly from the person they've always known.)

      SANDRA: Linda, why don't you bring Poppy next time?

      LINDA: Thanks Sandra, I'm not allowed to have her on my own anymore, but they might not mind if you're all with me.

      JENNY: Do you want to come trampolinercise Linda?

      LINDA: Oh yes, I'd love that.

(Green Woman enters and begins singing the intro to 'Shoes'.)

      ANNE: Come on, I'll take you back and we'll get ice cream – would you like that?

      LINDA: I wish you'd stop fussing Anne!

(The whirlwind begins again as they all say goodbye to one another and go off to their cars.)

      GREEN WOMAN: *(Sings.)*
      'Sometimes I'm 25,
      that woman never leaves.
      Sometimes I'm even 5,
      that little girl who still believes.
      I've been travelling a long time now
      and whatever path I choose
      I do it in every pair of shoes.

My soul is all the ages,
the feelings I have shown.
That's why I'm just 15 today
and all that kid had known.
I know how hard it is
to run a family and a home,
and to kick a ball
over next door's wall;
I've never really grown.

With all those girls here with me
I'm never gonna lose.
In every age I've ever been,
in every pair of shoes.
I'm all of the emotions
that a woman's ever known.
I'm 65 and I'm 25,
so young so old.
I'm so alive,
I yell it to the sky,
cos I'm only 5.
Every age I own;
I've never really grown.'

END

flapjackpress.co.uk